Times and Seasons

Writings from the Heart Of Maine

by
Write On! of People Plus

Times and Seasons
Writings from the Heart of Maine

An anthology of prose and poetry
by *Write On!* of People Plus in Brunswick, Maine

Copyright © 2014
by
The Authors of Write On! of People Plus

Other publications by Write On! of People Plus include:
Poets and Storytellers; Writing for fun
Poets and Storytellers; Writing for fun, volume II
It's About Time; Poems & Stories (CD) read by the authors
Muses and Memories; An Anthology of Prose and Poetry
From Maine and Away; An Anthology of Prose and Poetry

Cover design by Paul Karwowski
Cover Photographs by
Spring: Bonnie Wheeler
Summer: Paul Karwowski
Fall: Paul Karwowski
Winter: Gladys Szabo
Interior Drawings by Betty King
Introduction by Ruth Foehring

DEDICATION

This book is dedicated to those who love words and appreciate the skill, and sometimes magic, it takes to turn those words into something you'll never forget. We love sharing our words with each other in Write On! of People Plus, and now we're happy to share them with you.

ACKNOWLEDGEMENTS

A special recognition is in order for
the following members of Write On!

- Bonnie Wheeler for her steadfast leadership over the years.
- The wonderful and wicked "Sir Snidely" (Vince McDermott's alter ego) for his support over the years and keeping us on the straight and narrow while he goes elsewhere.
- Charlotte Hart, Bob Dow, Wendall Kinney, and Lynne Kresge for their many years and contributions to the group.
- Paul Karwowski and Ralph Laughlin for their efforts in the organization, editing, and publication of this book.

The Write On! group would also like to express its appreciation to Stacy V. Frizzle, Executive Director of People Plus, Frank Connors, Member Services Coordinator of People Plus, and the entire staff of People Plus for their past and continuing efforts on the Write On! group's behalf.

Table of Contents

Author/Title	Page
Charlotte Hart…………………………………………	1
My Grandfather…………………………………….	2
Sebago Lake on the Fourth of July…………………	3
Wedding in the Mountains of Stow, Maine………	4
Back to Boston—May 2013…………………………	5
Veterans Day and a Bike Chained to a Tree……….	6
The Deer Whisperer…………………………………	7
Brunswick in December……………………………	8
Where is Dave Slovenski? …………………………………	9
Ruth Foehring…………………………………………	11
The White Pigeon of Battery Park…………………	12
Together…………………………………………….	18
Bob Dow………………………………………………	22
What is Poetry? (and the Rhymer's Response)……	23
Signs of the Times…………………………………	24
People Watching (While on Parade)………………	25
The Bottom of the Fifth……………………………	26
Memorial Day………………………………………	26
Holiday Wishes to the WRITE ON! Group………	27
The Future………………………………………….	27
Bonnie Wheeler………………………………………	28
At Last…………………………………………….	29
Southern Comfort and Northern Bliss……………	30
Love Out Loud……………………………………	31
I Am……………………………………………….	31
Womankind………………………………………...	31
My Thursday Letter………………………………	32
Who Understands? …………………………………	33
Grandpa's Farm……………………………………	34
The Undecorated Tree……………………………	36
My Child …………………………………………	38
Sound Mind………………………………………	38
Elizabeth King………………………………………	39
Becoming Invisible………………………………	40
Heat of Crystallization……………………………	40

Table of Contents

Author/Title   **Page**

March Comes in ----	40
I Am	41
Grandmothers	42
Migration	43
The Leonids	44
Solstice	44
Dottie Moody	45
Write On	46
Sacred Space	47
Sermons or Poetry?	48
He's Beautiful	49
For This One Day	50
Peace	51
Kittie	52
To India	53
What Have I Done?	54
Lost Pictures	55
Time	56
Wendell Kinney	57
1941 Oldsmobile	58
Dunbar B & B	60
Oh, My Aching Back	63
Gladys Szabo	64
New Family Member	65
The Blizzard of 1977	66
Tribute to "My Dads"	68
Morning Serenity	69
The Accidental Hooker	70
Love at First Sight	71
Loving Memories of Aunt Ethel	72
Mother's Day Reflections	73
The Nest	73
Adelaide Guernelli	74
Thanksgiving Day	75
A Song I Heard in Maine	75

Table of Contents

Author/Title	Page
Life and Death..	75
Only One at a Time.....................................	76
Ann Robinson..	77
A Tail of Two Parents.................................	78
Doggone...	80
Spirit of Christmas.....................................	84
Ralph Laughlin..	85
Living in Maine...	86
I Can't Believe Everything I Know............	87
Math of Emotions......................................	87
I Think...	88
Conversation Between Two 21st Century Teens......	88
The Argument in Favor of Accumulative Materialism	89
Where Has America Gone...........................	90
The Twenty..	91
Party Politic Pox..	92
Ode to a Husband......................................	93
Spring..	94
Snowfall...	95
Ultimate Responsibility..............................	95
Nancy Sohl...	96
The Best Gift of All...................................	97
Remember When.......................................	98
The Little Things in Life............................	99
The Seasons of our Lives...........................	100
Camp Sunshine..	102
Snow Day..	103
Winnie Silverman.......................................	104
A Charming Old Cottage...........................	105
A Street Grows Up....................................	110
A Tree Grows in Cleveland.......................	111
Karen Schneider..	112
My Daughter, Kate....................................	113
The Sunday Tradition................................	114
Once..	115

Table of Contents

Author/Title	Page
A Summer Place…………………………………..	116
Vince McDermott…………………………………..	118
I Wrote a Poem………………………………..	119
Uncle Benny's Visit……………………………..	120
Cold Moonlight………………………………...	121
The Storm……………………………………...	122
Strawberry Season……………………………...	123
Groundhog……………………………………...	123
Be Careful What You Wish For………………...	124
The Adventures of Sir Snidely…………………	126
Karen Johnson……………………………………..	128
The Bear Who Came to My House…………….	129
Margie Kivel………………………………………..	131
A Day's Catch…………………………………..	132
Against the Gray……………………………….	133
Winter Candy…………………………………..	134
Cloud Dreaming………………………………..	134
Morning-After Ghosts………………………….	135
Step by Step……………………………………	136
October Flush………………………………….	137
Tell Me How You Came to Be…………………	138
Weekend Ritual………………………………...	139
Beth Compton……………………………………...	140
Bobby's Special Christmas…………………….	141
A Dark Stormy Night…………………………..	141
The Moonlit Night……………………………..	141
Penny the Sneaky Cat………………………….	142
Thanksgiving…………………………………..	142
What I Did When I was 25…………………….	142
The Little Girl's Christmas…………………….	143
The Dog and the Cat…………………………..	143
Paul Karwowski (P.K. Allen)……………………	144
The Seasons……………………………………	145
Spring…………………………………..	145
The Winds of Spring……………………	145

Table of Contents

Author/Title	Page
Summer	146
Summer Scenes	146
The Summer Wind	146
Fall	147
When Pine Needles Turn Brown	147
Winter	148
A Snowflake	148
Winter (a poem)	148
What I Like Most About America	149
My Bucket List	150
What If?	151
Letters	152
The Sands of Time	153
I Am	153
Wings	154
Sea of Love	154
Julia Garbowski	155
Milk	156
The Space Between	157
Cliché Woman	158
The Assentor	160
Patty Sparks	163
Haiku	164
The Messenger	164
Love and Longing	164
At Dawn	164
Butterfly Dancer	165
Untitled Dialogue	166
Winter Solstice	166
Twilight	167
Haiku from the Heart	167
The Decision	167
Roberta's Song	167
Seaweed	167
Autumnal Being	168

Table of Contents

Author/Title   **Page**

My "Maybe" View..	168
January..	169
Haiku for a Winter Soul...............................	169
Maine Nor'easter..................................	169
Winter Echo...	169
The Serenade...	170
Maine Summer Solitude...............................	171

INTRODUCTION

Within the covers of our book you will meet a variety of writers who have created stories and poems about many varied subjects. You will meet a young man receiving his first car and the lessons learned buying it. An old cottage and its history will enchant you as will the memory of a parade and an old veteran from the Civil War who waves at our writer when he was a child.

Experimenting with cigarettes at an early age ends with a stressful situation and a delightful story titled, "Remembering When," will get you thinking about times past. The memory of a boat built by a beloved grandfather is treasured. A tender story about "Two Dads" equally loved and fondly remembered, and a special great aunt and the joy of learning to sew with her, can only bring to mind people who have touched your life with love. A pigeon searching for adventure receives a surprise he is not prepared for. What if dogs took over and ruled and humans were expected to follow their rules? The amusing and clever poem, "Husband," says it all in five short sentences.

Colorful poems about the seasons in Maine will make you truly appreciate this great state, and an old letter from Dr. Jonas Salk adds to the list of interesting people met along the way. The birth of new born calves and the fight to keep some alive will touch and enthrall you. A poem about cloud formations will have you looking up in the sky for your own creative forms. Family traditions will bring back sweet memories of your own. A visit by a Mama bear and her cub will have you laughing out loud.

You will discover inspirational poems combined with words of wisdom written by playing with words until they reveal what they have to say. A cat named Penny, a dog named Rusty, a boy named Bobby, and a girl named Leah, will amuse and charm you. Words depicting love of God and country will find you appreciating this land and its people with a deeper regard.

Then you will find an unsavory character lurking in the shadows somewhere who adds unexpected humor to our book.

Lastly, clever Haiku and other poems provide pleasing visual and comforting word pictures to end our book. The covers close leaving lovely thoughts of a perfect summer day in Maine.

Charlotte Bourret Hart

Charlotte grew up in West Newfield, Maine. She graduated from Dean Academy in Franklin, Massachusetts, and the University of Maine at Orono. From 1957 through 2008, she lived and worked in Brunswick, Maine (Brunswick High School, Brunswick Junior High School, and part-time at Bowdoin College). She now resides in Cumberland, Maine. She writes personal narrative, character studies, light and humorous rhymed verse, and poetry inspired by life experiences, her late husband, her children, grandchildren, great grandchildren, and caring friends.

Charlotte Bourret Hart

MY GRANDFATHER

He built an inn on a tranquil lake
With gardens, pine breeze—heavenly!
He built an inn with a mountain view,
And he built a boat for me.

As a boy, he roamed Nova Scotia's shores,
Learned to work and to love the sea.
Life's journey was south to New England's towns.
And he built a boat for me.

A carpenter, forester, builder of homes
Screened porches, yards groomed carefully,
Multi-cropped gardens, paths, flat stepping stones.
And he built a boat for me.

He loved dogs—"Scot" and "Eppie", "Sweet-milk Buttercup",
Gentle draft horse "Ned Innesfree".
He taught me to love them, gently stroke their warm hair.
And he built a boat for me.

The boat was sturdy, safe, and strong
For the lake, the river, the sea,
For smooth safe travel my whole life long.
He built a boat for me.

Rock Haven Lake, West Newfield, Maine

Charlotte Bourret Hart

SEBAGO LAKE ON THE FOURTH OF JULY

The cottage is open. Soft lake breezes sigh.
Giant pines whisper welcome under Maine's bluest sky.
Be here on time. Before noon. You ask why?
Boat parade on the lake on the Fourth of July!

Speed boats! Row boats! Kayaks! A canoe.
Uncle Sam's barge. A house boat or two.
A flag flies from each vessel. Red, white, and blue!
The boat house sports bunting, patriotic and new.

On Uncle Sam's barge—musicians! A band.
Trumpets. Banjos. A joyful noise reaches land.
Elizabeth and her cousins march on the sand.
"It's a grand old flag," they shout back. Simply grand!

Ice cream we are making in the old cottage churn.
It won't take much longer. Each child takes a turn.
We'll have barbecued chicken, juicy steak for to die!
Then smooth white ice cream on three-berry pie.

Evening will come. To a great day good-bye.
Fireworks on the island will light up the sky.
From sleeping porch cots, we'll hear loons' soothing cry.
Under star-spangled heavens on the Fourth of July.

Charlotte Bourret Hart

WEDDING IN THE MOUNTAINS OF STOW, MAINE

We gather by a towering mountain range,
Friends, families with heartfelt joy impending.
Poems and songs prepare transference, change.
Air lock of vows leads to a knot unending.
Two single gems combine with mighty rope—
The loves of learning, gardening, preserving,
Exploring river, forest, sea—with hope,
They race together, determined and en-nerving!
Alaskan Malamute Juneau's dignified revue,
A joyous howl echoes! Gentle beast
Frees the throng to find a garden new,
A fine old home, a barbecue style feast.
The rhapsody of singing, celebration,
Warm toasts, and dancing end a day of sweet elation.

Charlotte Bourret Hart

BACK TO BOSTON – MAY 2013

I will go back to Boston.
Nothing will keep me away.
I'll walk the Common, watch the swan boats
As sun softens new leaves in May.

I will go back to Boston,
Join the crowd at old Fenway,
Sing "Sweet Caroline" by the diamond.
Nothing will keep me away.

I will shed a tear on Boylston Street
Then walk to the old North End.
Gallaria Umberto calzones will be lunch.
Then the Freedom Trail we will wend.

Harvard teams will row on the Charles.
Rowes Wharf boat? We'll take one for a day.
Go to and return from Nantasket Beach.
Nothing will keep me away.

The Boston Pops and fireworks
Stir the heart and fill the sky.
I will go to Boston to listen
On the night of the Fourth of July.

Charlotte Bourret Hart

VETERANS DAY
and a Bike Chained to a Tree

Before a young man left home to fight in World War I, he chained his bike to a tree. He never returned home.

Young Nelson fought the War to End All Wars,
Fierce World War I—that mankind might be free.
The Treaty of Versailles proclaimed a shaky peace.
Nelson had left his bike chained to a tree.

World War II raged—man's darkest—finest hour.
Pearl Harbor Day will live in infamy.
Our Youth, our Greatest Generation fought.
Hiroshima waged peace. The bike stood by the tree.

Cold War dragged on for long uneasy years.
U.S.S.R. dissolved eventually.
Our country called itself "sole super power".
Young Nelson's bike stayed chained to the growing tree.

Korean War, "Forgotten War", next surged.
Demilitarize a zone. That is the key.
Then Vietnam—years of defeat and rage.
Sad veterans bore shame. The bike stayed in the tree.

The Gulf War—Operation Desert Storm.
The War on Terror—Nine Eleven travesty,
The Taliban! Hussein! Bin Laden fell.
Is there promise from that bike chained to the tree?

Charlotte Bourret Hart

THE DEER WHISPERER

A steady gentle rain fell. The windshield wipers were rhythmic, slow. Cows grazed in the field to my right. People flocked the farm stand to my left, and I drove by slowly. I approached a lovely old set of buildings—the house attached to the barn which stood very close to the road. Suddenly! From behind that barn! Right in front of me! Two deer! I swerved. I avoided the big one; I hit the smaller one. I pulled off the road. Lights off. Wipers off. Umbrella. Keys. Don't lock yourself out! A truck coming south stopped. A young man and a boy about eight jumped out and ran to the wounded deer.

"Easy, fella, easy. You'll be okay. Mam, are you all right?"

"I'm all right," I breathed. The man and his son eased the deer off the road to the side of the barn. They settled it under a hydrangea. "It's okay, fella. It's all right. You'll be all right." His voice was soft, tender, as if he were speaking to a hurt child.

"Mam, I think it may be just a broken leg."

"Can we take him to Gray, Dad?"

"I'd like to, Bobby. Mam, I'd put him in my truck and take him to Gray Animal Farm, but I've got my dog with me. Wouldn't work."

A man in a yellow slicker came from the house across the road. He was speaking into his cell phone, "She seems all right. Her car looks okay. Yes. Yes." He closed his phone. "That was 911. They're sending help."

The boy and his dad kept soothing the deer. The beautiful animal lifted its head. Enormous brown eyes gazed at the young man who kept saying, "You'll be all right. You'll be all right."

This...this man...is a Deer Whisperer, I marveled.

Police arrived. Cars eased by. Blue lights were flashing. "Are you all right, Mam? Are you sure? Let's take a look at your vehicle. Turn the lights on. Signal lights. Don't see any damage. You were so lucky!"

"Yes," I told him, "if I had been going a tad faster, I'd have hit the big one. Is it okay if I go along now?"

"Stay a few minutes. Trooper may have questions. You can wait in your car."

"I like the fresh air." I opened my umbrella.

Charlotte Bourret Hart

The Trooper arrived. More blue lights were flashing. The Deer Whisperer and his son headed for their truck, "Come on, Bobby, we've done all we could do."

The Trooper was very tall, very dark, dark hair, dark eyes. "Are you okay, Mam? Step away, folks. Over there. Bullets can ricochet off a building." He drew his gun. The shot echoed from the side of the barn. The Trooper saw me wipe away a tear. "The meat will go to a needy family, Mam."

"That is…a…good thing," I sighed.

BRUNSWICK IN WINTER

Snow and ice. Cold sun. Bright night lights. December—
In Brunswick by the River—a month to remember.
Winter scenes were myriad, nostalgic to recall—
Laughter. Blades flashing. Skates gliding on the mall

Lessons and Carols greet the joyous season.
Ecumenical clergy—yearly—share treasured words of reason.
A ten-choir chorus! Saint John's Church. Magnificent!
Cornils' soaring music—such a gift. Beneficent!

Lighted lofted trees lined our long Maine Street.
Dancing elves in Senter's window bright verses would repeat.
They cheered wending lines of shoppers galore.
Downtown shopping mecca—Senter's fine old store.

Festivals at Bowdoin! Celebrations take flight.
Hanukkah! Kwanzaa! Christmas! Seasons of Light.
Precious stay—student years with future renown.
And chapel bells chime from the quad to the town

Charlotte Bourret Hart

*A Conversation, Winter of 2006-2007
at the Farley Field House Monitor's Desk at Bowdoin College*

WHERE IS DAVID SOLVENSKI?

"Mam, how much longer will this track meet go on?"

"Looks as if this one will end after midnight."

"Is this unusual?"

"Yes! This is a big one. Usually these high school meets are over between 10:30 and 11:00."

"We came to see the Slovenski boy in the pole vault. What's his name? Dan?"

"Dave. Dave Slovenski."

"I understand he is the son of the track coach here at Bowdoin."

"Yes. Dave is Coach Peter Slovenski's second son."

"Well! The pole vault has been going on for a while! Where is Dave Slovenski?"

"Look way down to the far end of the field house. See the Brunswick High team in black and orange, on the bleachers way at the end. See the boy sitting on the floor. That is Dave. Waiting. It will be a while before he can compete. These kids vaulting now are clearing 13 feet. Dave will probably clear 15 feet."

"Wow! It probably helps to have his father a track coach."

"It does not hurt."

"Does Coach Slovenski have special expertise in the pole vault?"

"Peter Slovenski set a Kennebec Valley Athletic Conference pole vault record in high school. That record held for over 30 years."

"Wow. Who broke that record?"

"Steve Slovenski."

"Another son?"

"Steve is Coach Slovenski's oldest son. Last February, Steve broke his dad's record and won the pole vault state championship. I saw him do that. That was at Slovenski Track at Bates."

"Slovenski Track? Wait a minute!"

"Yes. Slovenski Track was named after Walter Slovenski."

"Coach Slovenski's brother?"

"No. Coach Slovenski does have a brother who is a track coach—at M.I.T. Walter Slovenski was their father. One of my favorite Slovenski stories is about how Walter Slovenski got started in track. He grew up in Pennsylvania. When he finished 8th grade, he quit school and went to work in the coal mines. One Sunday afternoon he and his family were at a church picnic. There were games and races. A track coach saw Walter Slovenski run! He talked Walter's parents into having him return to school—and go out for track. Walter was in the service in World War II, and he went to college on the G.I. Bill. He was track coach at Bates for many years."

"I guess Slovenski men make a lot of headlines."

"Actually, the most Slovenski headlines I have seen were about Ruth Slovenski."

"Coach Slovenski's daughter?"

"No—his mother! Oh there she is now! She just came into the lobby. See the little lady with wavy gray hair? Running up the stairs."

"What did she do to make headlines?"

"She had her bicycle stolen."

"What?"

"Yes. She went to visit a friend in a nursing home. Didn't lock her bike. When she came out, it was gone. She told the police it had great sentimental value, a gift from her parents. She had been riding that bike for 66 years. It was written up in the Times Record. The Portland Press Herald. Boston papers! New York papers. Miami, San Francisco, Seattle. Everywhere in between. **'Eighty-three year old Maine woman has bicycle stolen'.**

Oh! Dave Slovenski is on his feet. He is starting to warm up. It is almost show time."

P.S. Dave Slovenski cleared 15' that evening, or rather at about 1:00 the next morning.

P.P.S. Because of the nationwide firestorm of publicity, the police were able to recover Ruth Slovenski's bicycle.

Ruth Foehring

Ruth was born in New York City in the borough of Queens, on Long Island. She attended Fordham University for two years where she met her husband, Bob. While raising four children, she attended night college for six years, received her degree, and began her teaching career.

Ruth and Bob lived in Vermont for thirty years, Florida for twelve, and summered in Maine since 1976. They bought a summer home in Phippsburg in 2000 and moved there from Florida in 2007. In October 2013 they moved to Topsham, Maine, where they have decided to live year round. They are now in the busy process of settling in.

Ruth writes mostly memoirs. They are all true stories that had an unforgettable impact on her. She is a story teller who focuses on interesting and amusing events experienced during her life

THE WHITE PIGEON OF BATTERY PARK

April had finally arrived, and at last spring had come to Battery Park in New York City. Patches of green grass on the lawn were noticed by people rushing to their various places of employment, and it seemed to be a welcome color. Many stopped to look at it and smiled as they hurried on. Under a long wooden bench sat a mound of snow that had once been bright white, but today it looked filthy and rejected and almost glad that it would take on a new form and disappear.

The birds had started to return a week earlier. They had sensed the passing of winter before most observers were aware of it leaving. They mingled in flight with the pigeons that had never forsaken the city, but had survived the winter with their own skills of endurance and patience.

The pigeons knew that the change of the season meant a big change for them. The park would soon be filled with people, and people meant popcorn. It also meant pieces of wonderful delicacies found in paper bags that these people carried each day to their favorite park benches.

The next day the sun shone longer and the winds coming across the Hudson River felt friendly and warmer. A cement path ran close to the river's edge and on nice days was always crowded with people. They seemed to enjoy the ripples in the water and loved watching the boats that continually passed by.

By noon the park actually seemed over crowded. The past months it had been deserted and so it indeed seemed right to be mobbed with people. The food stand at the corner of the park had resumed business, and the aroma of food cooking drifted over the paths and benches.

The pigeons waited for someone to begin sharing his lunch, then flew to that spot and began waddling over the ground. They soon were rewarded and their daily routine was set.

The pigeons came in a variety of colors. Gray heads mingled with black, white, and brown ones. Their feathers contrasted with their bodies and together in a group they formed a mass of color. People seeing the group one day would fail to recognize any one pigeon that stood out from the rest, at least not until the third week of spring!

A pure white pigeon with a purple smudge under his left eye made his appearance that week on a dismal Monday morning. His whiteness contrasted with the gray sky and the high buildings that lay across from the park. He seemed eager and hungry and pushed his way among the other pigeons with a lively enthusiasm. The other pigeons observed his bad manners and gave him lots of feather room. It was not acceptable to butt into a particular territory uninvited and proceed to eat everything in sight.

The white pigeon was always hungry. Perhaps because he was larger than most of the pigeons, he had to consume more food, or maybe it was because of his greedy personality. He never lasted very long in one group and always had to move on to find a new part of the park to satisfy his appetite.

Tuesday was a glorious day and many people came to the park. Popcorn, bits of doughnuts, cookies, waffles, sugar cones, and bologna sandwiches were everywhere. The white pigeon feasted and thought this park must surely be the very best of places to live. He decided to remain here forever.

Home Sweet Home!

He found himself a lovely place to rest and spend his nights and called this his home. It was located on the fifteenth floor of a steamship company, and it was located right across the street from the park. It had a perfectly gorgeous view of the Hudson River. The spot he had chosen was a sheltered and secluded corner of a very wide window ledge. It had a nice overhang that provided warmth and kept him dry when it rained.

The morning sun warmed the ledge for many days, and then the weather changed. The rain began to fall and the temperature dropped abruptly. The white pigeon was indeed glad that he had found his comfortable corner, for a big change was taking place in his life and one he did not particularly care for.

The park was empty and as the unpleasant weather continued, the park remained a vacant and dreary place. People were staying in their buildings and not venturing into the park to relax.

The pigeon was miserable and hunger finally forced him to search out a new food supply. He was reduced to searching in garbage heaps and to digging up worms which he detested. He yearned for a sunny day to return.

A New Friend Appears!

He had noticed the sea gulls flying out to the river when he had first arrived. They would venture into the park too, but lately they were never around. They formed massive specks of white dots in the sky that swerved and dived.

One day the white pigeon flew back to his ledge only to find a young sea gull sitting there. The gull still had many brown feathers indicating his youth. He was friendly and began to chat immediately. "The weather sure has been terrible these past two weeks," said the sea gull in a cheery voice.

"I don't see how you can be so pleasant about it," said the pigeon. "I am hungry and have not seen the sun in so long. I miss all the joy of living by this park."

"Hungry?" asked the sea gull. "Why there is no need for that. Fly with me to the ferries! You will be delighted with the flight and there is food on those boats. People seem to like seeing us darting over their heads. They throw food up in the air and we dive down and snatch it up. It's fun and it's breakfast, lunch, and dinner. You really do not have to fly up with me, but just walk around on the deck of the boat and get all that falls to the ground."

The white pigeon gazed out over the dreary city, saw the river in the distance, and envisioned his lunch and his mind was made up. "I would like to join you. It sounds great to me!"

The two left the ledge and their graceful bodies soared through the air. As they approached the river, the air became cooler, and the sound of tooting horns and boat motors was very apparent. Something stirred in the pigeon, and he felt as if a new and exciting world was about to open up for him.

A New Character is About to Change Everything!

In the meantime, another episode was taking place that would affect the life of the pigeon in a most peculiar manner. Mario Bonfiglio, an unemployed father of six children was about to embark on a ferry voyage across the river. It was his second trip across that day, and he was returning home an unhappy man. He had gone to New York, seeking work but had been told that none was available.

He walked up the gang plank with determined steps. If one was to observe him carefully they would notice he was carrying three burlap bags. They were carefully folded under his left arm.

He walked to the top deck and stood there staring out over the water. He searched the sky as if looking for something and then sat down and awaited the ship's departure. He didn't seem to mind the slight drizzle and cool air. He relaxed, the ship moved, he stroked the bags on his knees and waited.

The boat moved slowly and evenly out into the deeper, blue water. The passengers stayed indoors and looked out of the glass enclosed cabin. Some read newspapers or books while others talked, but most sat quietly and thought about their day or what the day still had in store for them. The coffee and doughnut stand began a busy business.

Out to the Boats!

The gull and the pigeon approached the ferry. They flew over two ferries, but no one was out on the deck so they circled and flew over a third. They noticed one lone man sitting quietly. They were about to leave when they saw him leave his seat and walk over to the rail. He took out a small paper bag and began eating something from it. The birds decided to remain in hopes of receiving something from that bag.

Mario deliberately did not look up. He was remembering days gone by, days from his childhood. He envisioned a small house in a faraway country. His father was cooking on an outdoor stone grill. On the grate baking were six small skinned birds. This would be dinner that evening, and the family eagerly awaited it.

The ferry horn tooted and the vision faded. A new one took its place and he saw his own family. A wife and six children sat hungry at an empty table. That night he would provide a dinner that would be delicious and not tax his empty wallet.

The gull flew down and circled the man. He threw crumbs into the air, and the gulls darted and caught the morsels in midair. This action was repeated many times. The pigeon watched and decided to try his luck too.

Mario knew what he must do. He threw a large square piece of bread up in the air and many bits and pieces of the same on the deck. The gull flew for the large square, and the pigeon flew to the deck. He strutted about and picked up many of the bits slowly and with little caution. Mario in a flash was upon the unsuspecting white pigeon. A bag was thrown over the pigeon. The next instant the pigeon was grabbed by the neck by a powerful hand. The other hand jerked open the bag. The pigeon was thrown inside, and the bag was tightly closed with a piece of old clothesline.

The pigeon was terrified. The bag was dark. Some light and air did penetrate through the woven burlap bag, but he still felt that his air supply was being cut off with every passing second.

The gull wondered where his friend had disappeared to. He flew over the boat twice, shrugged his wings and decided to try elsewhere. He could not ever have imagined what fate had struck his former companion.

A Shocking Observation!

A passenger traveling on the ferry walked to the window and stared out. She was hoping to see a change in the weather and a bit of blue in the sky. Mrs. Maloney took the ferry once a week to attend school in a downtown New York college that offered classes

on Saturdays. She was now on her way home to New Jersey. She looked to the left of the vacant deck and saw a man with a sack throwing food into the air. On the ground nearby were other sacks. One seemed to be producing movement within its boundaries. The bag's sides were pushing out and bulged in different positions.

As she watched, the man's actions had seemed to interest a brown pigeon, and he flew down to the deck. What happened next came as a complete surprise to the totally shocked woman. The pigeon was grabbed quickly and deposited into the sack. A rope was tied to enclose the bird, and the bag was thrown on the deck. Now two bags jumped on the deck.

Mrs. Maloney opened the door and found herself flying across the deck. "What are you doing?" she demanded!

"Mind your own business lady. Go back inside where you came from and just leave me alone!"

The horn of the boat sounded. The trip was coming to an end. People began appearing on the deck. Before she could respond the man grabbed the one empty sack and the two filled ones and hurried down the nearest stairs.

She knew she could do nothing and sadly watched as the boat was carefully docked. She saw the man get off the boat and disappear into the crowded port.

That night a family enjoyed a pigeon stew, and that night Mrs. Maloney told her family a story that they refused to believe.

TOGETHER

The afternoon was fading, and the streetlights came on softly and blazed in circles of comforting light. Susanne stood before the large plate glass windows in front of her and watched the cars passing by. The beams of their headlights seemed to reach out and touch the cars ahead of them. People hurried by, and a few glanced in her direction and smiled.

Susanne had had a busy day! The position of assistant manager of a Singer Sewing shop in a small town in Vermont had been particularly exhausting all week. Halloween was around the corner, and it seemed as if every mother in town was preparing to make the costume that would win the grand prize at the local grammar school. She was an excellent seamstress, enjoyed sewing, was very content selling sewing machines and supplies, and liked giving instructions and advice to the women who flocked into the shop six days a week.

Ten months from now she would marry. She and Tom had purchased a condo and would move in right after their honeymoon. They had fallen in love with the small homey dwelling at first sight. The rooms, however, would remain empty if they did not start ordering furniture. Furniture store customers were always told that it took many months for delivery, so she was anxious to begin the hunt. It was five thirty and time to close the shop and leave. Surveying the shop and pleased that all was in order, she put her coat on, turned the light off and locked the door.

Tonight she would not go straight home. She had made an appointment for six o'clock. Susanne hurried to her car and drove off in the direction of her meeting. She felt a twinge of anxiety and hoped all would go well. An ad in the Help Wanted section of the Free Press had jumped right out at her. A sewing teacher was wanted. The hours were wonderful, from six to nine and only twice a week. The words that had caused the anxiety were that the teacher was needed at the "Women's Correctional Center." Her mother was appalled that she would even consider it, "Please reconsider. It is not worth the money and could be dangerous." She hadn't listened, but those words were now ringing in her ears!

The brick building, ablaze with lights, loomed in front of her. She told the guard at the gate of her scheduled appointment. He checked his book, opened the gate, and she drove in. She parked the car and walked to the entrance. A box was next to the door. It read, "Push button and speak into the intercom." A deep voice spoke up at once, "Please state your business." She responded and the door swung open.

A guard met her inside, inspected her purse and pockets and escorted her down a long hall. The hall floor was waxed, and the walls were white and looked like they had recently been painted. They made their way silently and stopped before an office door. The interview was about to begin.

The guard knocked on the door, a voice replied, and Susanne entered the room. A small woman with a kind face and graying hair motioned that she be seated. Questions were asked and answered, and she was hired quickly. They would expect her every Tuesday and Thursday. Susanne asked where the teaching would take place, and she was taken to a room that reminded her of the boy's shop room in high school. The sewing machines were still in boxes in a far corner, but she was assured all would be in its proper place when she arrived the following week.

Susanne was asked to make a list of the articles she required and leave it off as soon as possible. She thought that the prison had a college dorm atmosphere except for the guards scattered here and there. There were no bars in view, and she had even passed a cozy day room with flowered covered couches, a fish tank and a large television. The interview had gone well, and she now had a week to worry about what she had agreed to!!

Ruth Foehring

Lesson Time

It was Tuesday and it was time to begin. The women filed into the room, and Susanne observed them carefully. There were ten of them, and they ranged in age from around eighteen to perhaps fifty. They were dressed in sweaters and sweatshirts and jeans and seemed friendly and not at all life threatening. A guard could be seen through the glass on the door. This helped boost Susanne's confidence. Her knees stopped shaking and her heart beat to a better rhythm. The inmates seated themselves behind ten green tables. On each was a new sewing machine. Susanne introduced herself and told them what her goals were for the following months. Then she went to the blackboard and began drawing and teaching. These lessons and instructions were to last a full year.

Needles, patterns, material, and thread were passed out. They were all going to make an apron, but later each could decide what they would prefer to make. Susanne had the only pair of scissors in the room, so getting started was slow and time consuming.

She now looked forward to Tuesday and Thursday nights. It was a joy to watch the progress of her students. Everyone made something, A few showed talents they would pursue in the future. One would become a seamstress and earn a living sewing because of Susanne's visits. Another made her wedding dress with Susanne's considerable assistance and direction.

Susanne had become a devoted teacher. Her pupils grew to admire and respect her. She earned the money needed to buy the luxuries that were unaffordable before and ordered her furniture.

Ruth Foehring

Time Marches On

Driving home from work four years later, Susanne stopped at the local A & P for a few groceries. She and Tommy were going bowling after supper. She quickly collected the items on her list and placed them in her shopping cart. Each item was carefully counted, and when she had reached ten, she stopped. Ten or less was the magic number one needed to go through the fast checkout lane!

The line at the checkout was unusually long, but she knew it would move quickly. She got on the end of the line and waited. Recognizing people in her small community, she greeted them with a smile or a wave. Her minister's wife was two places ahead of her and directly behind her was her mother's next-door neighbor. Members of her church, people on her bowling league, and customers from the shop, were on adjacent lines.

The line did not move quickly, and Susanne began to wonder if some people had more than the ten items allowed. It would be most disturbing if someone she knew was the culprit, or even worse, culprits. She hoped it was not the minister's wife!!

She was about to start checking on this when she noticed a large woman in another line but not recognizing her, she neither smiled nor waved.

Susanne had a faint recollection of the woman, but where they had encountered each other in the past did not surface immediately. She stared blankly at the face before her.

The face suddenly fit into place. It was a familiar scene, really unforgettable, but had not been thought of in quite a while. There in vivid color was a green desk. Sitting before it was this very woman, and on that very table was a sewing machine.

Susanne's mouth opened, but no words were even faintly uttered. Her eyes opened wide and stared in horror as she and everyone else heard, "Susanne, Susanne.........don't cha remember me! We was in Prison together!!!!

The telephones rang that night.... all over town!!!

Bob Dow

Bob grew up in Melrose, Massachusetts. He attended MIT for a degree in engineering and economics, and then served in the Army in France during the Korean War. Bob married the late Elaine Erskine, and they raised two daughters. When he retired from financial work, twenty years ago, he moved to Brunswick, Maine.

Bob's pastimes have included family, photography, rhyming verse, and computer graphics supporting **Write On!** of People Plus. He has a travelogue of Alaska and a few magazine covers to his credit, and also a brief stint as an extra in a PBS historical drama.

Bob Dow

WHAT IS POETRY?
(and the Rhymer's Response)

I'm not the right person to ask,
Although I will give it a try.
Defining it is quite a task,
Without the results being dry.

From Webster, my number one source:
A metrical writing or verse,
The work of a poet, of course,
For whom writing isn't a curse.

An image, our words should create:
Descriptive and also appealing.
Emotion, one wants to relate:
Evocative, with lots of feeling.

A writing that certainly formulates
A given emoti'nal awareness
In language that's chosen and concentrates:
Specific and certn'ly not careless.

The language then should be poetic,
About an experience or feeling:
Descriptive, not weak but aesthetic;
Above all it should be revealing.

Now, what I compose are not 'pomes'—
They're more a Thalian-type beast.
In my verse, some jokes will find homes.
Thank God for a giggle at least.

SIGNS OF THE TIMES

I'd almost forgotten those signs
Placed out in front windows by Mum.
Now, one was for *Cushman* to stop,
And one caused the ice man to come.

No sign for the coal man these days
Who had to deliver by bag.
No way was the coal chuted in—
Recall, though, the dust made us gag.

We fin'ly converted to oil,
But, back to the coal during war.
In winter the milk came by sleigh,
Or else I would ski to the store.

The scissor-man pushed his small cart—
One more who no longer survives.
I still can imagine those bells
That told us to take out our knives.

The trolley: replaced by a bus.
The tracks played a wartime steel roll.
The elm, of course, no longer there:
A '38 hurricane toll.

Those images out of the past
Still vivid—though I must confess:
Today's assigned task—I forgot.
A sign of the times, I would guess.

Bob Dow

PEOPLE WATCHING
(While on Parade)

For many years I marched
In uniforms—some starched—
A long time it has been.
A drummer I was then.

The last group that I played with*
(And this is not a myth)
Was twenty drummers strong—
And we could thrill a throng.

The drums, it should be mentioned:
Colonial, rope-tensioned.
No question we were loud,
But we could please the crowd.

I liked to scan that crowd
(To see if they'd been wowed).
Our drumming—an attraction—
I watched for their reaction.

Who were the most excited?
The girls—they were delighted.
They were the ones who raved.
They danced and clapped and waved.

No use to go on crowing,
Much older we kept growing.
Those were the good old days—
Recalled, now, through a haze.

*Linn Village Drum Band, Wakefield, Massachusetts

Bob Dow

THE BOTTOM OF THE FIFTH

The television wason
The *Yankees* versus *Sox*.
So far, so good, because
The score: two runs, two walks.

Now, everything was dandy.
The game was going well—
The whiskey bottle handy.
The outcome? Time would tell.

But then the mood was breached.
Our joy became a myth,
And all because we'd reached
The bottom of the fifth.

MEMORIAL DAY
Or Mr. Robinson's last Parade

When I was very young—and that's some time ago,
A memory stands out. I don't know why that's so.
It was *Memorial Day*, and a parade went by.
I loved the marching bands—and maybe that is why.
What I remember, though, is not the marching feet,
Nor list'ning to the music with its martial beat.

An open car passed by containing one old man.
He waved to me, I thought, as if I were a fan.
But who was he? I asked. Dad said, "There are no more;
He is the last in town who fought the Civil War."
I was so young it didn't mean a thing, you see,
And yet—I still recall that Vet'ran's wave to me.

HOLIDAY WISHES
to the WRITE ON! Group

To a great group of folks,
Who do not mind my jokes
And the things that I write
That are not all that bright.

T'is the end of the year
And it's time for good cheer.
So to each of you now:
Here's a wish from Bob Dow

Happy Yuletide of course,
That's a wish I'll endorse,
And again, not in jest,
For the New Year: The Best!

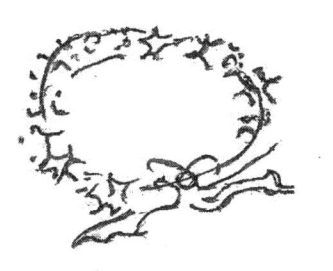

THE FUTURE

I've long since passed my sell-by date.
I haven't a clue what's due from fate.
If I could look into a glass
And see what all will come to pass,
I'm sure I couldn't stand the stress.
I'll stick with day by day I guess.

Bonnie Wheeler

Bonnie shares her love of writing with People Plus and Word Weavers of the Topsham literary writing groups. She writes in a variety of styles; true and fiction stories, plays, free verse, and poetry. Bonnie published two novellas in 2013; *Without My Toothbrush, and Mama's Pies.*

She grew up on the plains of Oklahoma where having a little was a lot. She is blessed to be a Navy wife and mother of three, grandmother of eight, and great-grandmother of two. She lives each day grateful for God's grace and favor.

Bonnie Wheeler

AT LAST

In 1964, we were stationed in San Diego, California, a Navy family with two young sons. Gary's orders sent him to the USS Constellation. The ship was headed for the Gulf of Tonkin, the start of the Vietnam War. The first fighter airplane shot down was from that ship. Its pilot was captured and became the first POW.

The war did not go as Americans expected. Political influence and lack of American support prolonged a long and horrific war. 58,220 soldiers died and many others were left mentally and physically impaired. We left Vietnam without a victory.

When Gary returned home, it was not to a hero's welcome but to a mostly uncaring nation. Only the soldiers who served, and their families, knew and grieved for the ones who had given their all. At last the broken and beaten POWs would return to a small joyful reunion with their families and fellow soldiers. Often when asked where they had been for the past years, and answering Vietnam, they would be greeted with silence and disappointment, and even hostile words.

The military continued the job of serving and protecting America, seldom hearing the words, "thanks for serving," or "well done." Vietnam veterans were grateful to be alive and back home. Time passed, retirement from the Navy, children grew, grandchildren born, we moved on – 50 years.

This week Gary went to Portland to eat out at Cracker Barrel, and after a good meal the check came paid in full with these written words, **"Thank you for your service."**

He was shocked and amazed and wondered how they knew. Then he realized his ball cap said, **Vietnam Veteran**. At age 75, it was a satisfying feeling to at last be appreciated.

Bonnie Wheeler

SOUTHERN COMFORT AND NORTHERN BLISS

Southern folks sit on front porches and invite neighbors to join them after a Sunday dinner of fried chicken, cream gravy, biscuits – hot and buttery, fried okra, and perhaps banana pudding for dessert. Northern folks eat hotdogs and beans for Saturday night dinners and fish chowder for lunch, sitting in their kitchen, with wood stoves warming their toes.

Where do I belong, after years of growing up in the south and now retired in the north? My mind hasn't adjusted to all the changes, often thinking, "Is this where I should be?" At times, I yearned for the familiar warmth of true Southern hospitality. The smiles and greetings to everyone – doesn't matter if you know them or will ever see them again – it's a sweet courtesy given freely. I miss the southern gentlemen rushing to open doors for you, answering questions with "Yes, ma'am," and removing their cowboy hats in your presence. I miss large, spirit-filled churches with people greeting friends or strangers with "God bless you, honey," or "Come see us…you know you could," and you would receive a welcome. Mostly, I miss the wisdom and advice and love shared on front porches.

I think of fall in New England when God splashes colors that you cannot capture with a paintbrush or a camera. When I drink a cold glass of apple cider and delight in the experience, I know this special treat cannot be found in the South. I think of toasty, dreamy flames spreading warmth around the room from a fireplace, a kitchen table where families spin yarns of past winters when wet snow was so high no one could get to the barns. I think of asking who shot a deer for their winter's meat, or what's going on at the Grange Hall, and who's going to the bean supper on Saturday? Northern folks are happy and satisfied in their little piece of heaven.

I love each place and feel blessed to have experienced a taste of Southern comfort and Northern bliss. I am thankful and grateful that God allowed me to live in both places – a special gift.

Bonnie Wheeler

LOVE OUT LOUD

I would like to learn to love out loud
So loud that others could see it
So loud that others could feel it
Sharing spirit energy with the world
Spreading love, peace, and beauty
Willing others to stop and listen
    Paying it forward everyday

I AM

I am nothing to most
Everything to some
Grateful for the journey
I trust who I am
A miracle design of dust
By the one and only – I Am

WOMANKIND

Insight just brushed my thoughts.
A mother and daughter's tears
travel the same path.
Future generations, similar faces
shedding tears in different places.

Bonnie Wheeler

MY THURSDAY LETTER

"Look what I found behind the file cabinet in the basement," said my husband. He handed me a yellowed envelope. My heart started beating faster. The letter was from my mother who had passed away years ago. The postmark was 1986 with a $.22 stamp. My hands shook as I held this gift. Mother wrote each of her children a letter every Sunday afternoon. We all lived, worked and raised our children in different parts of the country, California, Arkansas, Kansas City, Oklahoma, and Maine. Mother kept us close with her letters telling us what was happening in each family. On Thursdays, I went to the mailbox and just like clockwork, there was a letter from my mother. Her sudden death of a heart attack left me feeling lost. No longer did I have a mother to advise me, to talk to, or return home to visit. There were no more letters in the mail on Thursdays and my connection was broken.

In my hand I held the last Thursday letter. I held the old dusty yellow envelope with reverence. Inside were my mother's words. She held the pen, addressed the envelope, licked the stamp, and shared her Oklahoma life with me. I had one last, lost letter to read, my Thursday letter. I carefully opened the envelope and out came six pictures taken on our trip to Bartlesville, Oklahoma to visit my youngest sister, Marsha. Mom said to keep two and send four to Marsha. In the picture, Marsha, her children and husband were all sitting in a sandbox playing. There were pictures of her house, the family cooking together, and a family reunion. It was a precious time. Sadly, I could not send them to Marsha. She died unexpectedly a year ago. I could send them to her husband and children. I believe they will be even more precious now.

Mother's letter told of an approaching storm. She hoped there wouldn't be any tornados so they wouldn't have to run to the dirt cellar. Dad was watching it as she wrote. She said she had worked in the garden that day weeding and a young neighbor came by and said, "Ruby, don't you have anything cooler to work in." The Oklahoma sun was beating down. She said," Well, no, I don't." The neighbor went to town and brought her a thin duster dress and wrote happy Mother's Day, though it really wasn't. Mother said what a sweet girl she was. She said her beans and peas were almost ready to bloom and hoped the coming storm would not ruin them, but the storm blew over and brought in cool winds. She loved that feeling.

She wrote that one grandson was sick and did not look healthy. She thought my sister was running her kids ragged and she needed to remember that kids get tired too. She said her daycare mother had two new babies coming in June for her to take care of. She said she was counting her chickens before they hatched, and that she had better wait to say that. She admitted she got too attached to her daycare kids.

The two rosebushes she planted weren't growing at all. The only thing that grew well in their dry Oklahoma dirt was cactus. She said to tell my son Kevin, whose wife was expecting a child, that grandmothers make more time for grandchildren. They have the time to see their beauty and appreciate more how much they mean to them.

She said my brother Donald can't come for a visit because too many of his cows are calving at the same time. She said her teeth needed to be relined and there wasn't anything funny about that. The dentist said he would do it for free, and then sent her a bill for $150. She called him and he said it was a mistake. She said it wouldn't have been if she had paid it. The letter ended, See you all – Mother and Dad.

So many memories flooded into my head. Mother, Dad, Marsha and Donald, all gone, yet a piece of their lives on in my Thursday letter.

WHO UNDERSTANDS?

Who understands when your mood is bad?
Who listens patiently when you are sad?
Who advises a new road to take?
Who waits at the dentist when your tooth aches?
Who mops the floor when you throw up?
Who says to your face that you need to grow up?

Even when angry, her love shows through,
Only a mother – that's who.

Bonnie Wheeler

GRANDPA'S FARM

School was out. I was going to Grandpa's farm. My grandpa was the wisest man I knew, and I loved spending time with him and my cousin Gaye. She was my partner to run wild through the farm field with. At sundown, Grandpa would send us with Lassie, his herd dog, to bring the cows to the barn. Lassie did most of the herding, and we ran and jumped pretending to be cowboys on a cattle drive, whipping a stick in the air like a lasso and yelling, "Get along little doggies," until we came to the block of salt, and like the cattle, we too took a big lick. We never heard of cow lick disease, so no problem.

The next day, we found a tall tree with a bird nest. We climbed up and saw there were tiny blue speckled eggs in it. We brought the nest down carefully to go show Grandpa. He looked at the eggs and told us they were Oklahoma scissortail bird eggs. We had seen those birds with the long sharp tails before. He said we were lucky because if the mother bird had caught us stealing her eggs, she would have cut our fingers off. Wide-eyed, we took the nest back and didn't bother it again, thankful to have all of our ten fingers. Grandpa just smiled and took another puff of his Camel cigarette.

A few days later, we took a pack of his cigarettes thinking it would be fun to learn to smoke. We took a handful of long wooden matches out of the box in the kitchen and ran out behind the barn. We lit up together and choked, coughed, and spat. We decided smoking was awful and not at all fun, and we didn't care for a second one. Now, what to do with the almost full pack? We buried it in a deep hole, went to the well, washed out our mouths, and went to supper.

Grandpa said, "Bonnie do you want to catch a bird? Bring the salt shaker, and if you can toss some salt on its tail, you can have it." Since I did want a bird, I went off to the front porch where the honeysuckle grew thick and that birds flew into. I began to sling salt. Again, Grandpa smiled and lit up a cigarette. Then he said," Last night, a rat got into my cigarette carton. It's okay because I had poisoned that pack." The salt shaker fell out of my hands. I looked at Gaye, and she back at me, terrified. We both ran to the back of the farmhouse and waited to die. We looked at the stars and moon and cried, thinking how our mothers would miss us. We went to bed and tried to keep each other awake until we fell asleep exhausted. We were so surprised to wake up the next morning we waited for several days to die. We finally decided it would probably take more than one cigarette to kill us. The experience kept us from ever wanting to try smoking again for the rest of our lives. Thank you, Grandpa, for never telling my folks about our misadventures.

At the end of my visit, he said, "Call your momma to see if you can stay longer." I ran to the old crank phone and cranked one short and two long and listened as everyone on the party line picked up. I begged Momma to let me stay. I said Grandpa needed me to help in the garden and to get the cows. She said, "Yes," and I ran to the porch, and smiling, climbed onto grandpa's lap. I was so content rocking, listening to the birds, petting Lassie, and smelling the sweet honeysuckle and Camel cigarette smoke. Life on Grandpa farm was sweet.

Bonnie and Grandpa on her wedding day in 1960.

Bonnie Wheeler

THE UNDECORATED TREE

His mama pushed him out the car door with his paper sack of clothes. She said, "It's your no good daddy's time to take care of you. I got my chance to go to Florida with my boyfriend and he don't want no extra garbage, like a kid. Go to apartment 43 and give him this letter. It is not that I don't care about you, Danny, I need my space, and this is my chance to go places." Danny looked at the strange neighborhood and put his hand out to open the door to get back in her car. His mama drove away real fast. He watched until she disappeared into heavy traffic.

He guessed he had better go find his daddy. He was glad his teacher, Miss Jane, had taught him to read. He liked Miss Jane. It made him sad not to be able to go to school anymore. Someone came out of the building and asked him if he was lost. He didn't know what to answer because he did feel lost. The man told him to go see the manager at the first door, and he did. The big heavy-set man said," What do you want kid?" Danny told him he was looking for his dad who lives in number 43. The man told him to go up the stairs and down the hall and get out of his sight. Danny headed in the right direction and wondered if he would know his dad. He had left them three years ago. Then he remembered the night he came home drunk, and his mama yelled at him to go away and not to come back. Then his mama cried and cried when he did. Big people are funny. Why was mama so upset when his dad did what she said? He hadn't missed his dad because he was always drunk and causing trouble. He sure hoped he had changed.

Standing in front of the door, he took a deep breath, set down his sack, and knocked on the door. Finally, a small girl opened the door and said, "What you want white boy?" He didn't know what to say, so he said nothing. The girl's mother yelled, "Who is it, Jenna," and then came to the door. She said," What do you want?" He told her he came to find his dad. "What's his name?" she asked. He replied, "Don Hicks." "Never heard of him. We've been living here going on two years. Go ask the manager," and she shut the door.

Danny was afraid to ask the manager anything and went to sit on the front steps to think about what to do. It was cold, so he decided to walk down the street. The smells coming from the bakery made him realize how hungry he was. He wished he had some money. Next door was a barbershop, so he decided to go in where it was warm, and to sit down for a while. The barber told him to sit down and that he would be with him in a minute, and went back to cutting hair. Danny needed to use the bathroom and saw a door going to the back room. He found the bathroom and a small kitchen and sitting room. He saw a tray of cookies and candy on the table. He thought if he ate a few he could spread the rest around and fill in the missing space. Oh, they were so good. Then he decided he would lie down for just a minute and rest there. He lay down and pulled the blanket over his head and fell sound asleep.

The barber asked Sam, his customer, where the boy went. Neither one of them had seen him leave. They decided that he must have. The barber said, "Sam, come over for Christmas. LeAnn is so sad since we lost Kevin. All she does is cry. She wants a child so badly. We are thinking about adoption. She still works with the cancer foundation and that helps. She cannot decorate a Christmas tree. She says, "What's the use and why would we bother? It is hard seeing all the old decorations of Kevin and Santa Claus each year." I guess I wonder the same thing, why bother, but it's time to start living again. She will appreciate the cookies and the peanut butter balls. No one can make them like Nichole, you tell her thanks so much. Dave walked Sam to the door, put the closed sign out, swept the floor, hung up his barber smock, and headed to the back to get the cookie tray and lockup for the holidays.

Tonight he would insist they decorate their tree which was standing in the corner of the living room. Please, God, help me find a way to ease LeAnn through this sorrow. Dave picked up the candy tray and out of the corner of his eye he saw the blue blanket move. Darn, that cat next door must have sneaked in and made a bed on his sofa. Well, he would go out faster than he came in. He jerked the blanket up and yelled, "Scat cat."

To his amazement, the missing boy from his shop looked back at him with a frightened look. Dave said, "Son, what in the world are you doing here? Your folks must be frantic with worry. Were you supposed to meet your dad here? No one came looking for you." Danny told him his story. Dave listened in disbelief. This child had no idea where his mother or father was. Dave noticed his eyes drifted to the cookies and realized he was hungry. He knew he should call the police and let them handle this unfortunate situation. He decided to wait until he fed him.

He asked Danny if he could eat a hamburger. Danny smiled in delight and said he thought he could eat two. Hand in hand they walked to the nearest café and put in an order for four hamburgers, French fries, and apple pies. The owner said, "What you got here, Dave? Did Santa bring you a helper for Christmas?" and laughed. Dave looked startled and did not laugh back. Under his breath he said, "Maybe he did."

Dave carried the bags of food and Danny carried the apple pie to a nice house. Dave went through the door and called out, "LeAnn, come see what Santa brought us to help decorate our tree."

MY CHILD

> I knock at heaven's door each day
> Ask help for the child I raised
> Take away hurts, hardships, and pain
> Bless their days, guard their ways
> God heard – looking at his own son
> Smiled and said, "Consider it done."

SOUND MIND

> The Bible says we are not given
> a spirit of fear but of power,
> love, and a sound mind.
>
> When I was young,
> it was all about love –
> finding that special someone.
>
> Later, it was all about power,
> raising children, careers,
> and making life work.
>
> Today, in my sunset years,
> It's all about a sound mind.
> **Lord, don't fail me now**.

Elizabeth King

Betty was born and raised on the Chicago North Shore (the Scarsdale of the West). She migrated east to school, and graduated from MIT with a degree in Architecture, with a major interest in solar and environmental design. She lived and worked in the Boston area until somewhere in the "fifties" when she discovered Maine, and retired "back to the land" to raise 8 children and many other things on a hardscrabble saltwater farm in Woolwich.

Betty started writing while homeschooling – by this time she says she actually had something to write about. She jumped back into professional activity in the "70"s prompted by the oil embargo which made solar design relevant once more, and worked for the DOE for a while on a project using holography to utilize sunlight for architectural lighting. She wrote the reports and proposals because she was the only one in the group who could type (this has gotten her into all kinds of trouble). Betty did passive-solar design as a sole practitioner in Maine for a while until she retired.

Today Betty enjoys writing, singing, gardening, playing with her grandchildren, doing lots of volunteer work, and enjoying her many friends.

Elizabeth King

BECOMING INVISIBLE

Crystals of ice, fragile, ephemeral, _
moisture of the soil, essential, invisible -
Beside the highway the rock face gathers glassy columns
which manifest the invisible element
so beautifully, in ice.
As the days lengthen, the sun's heat strengthens ---
the vision vanishes.

HEAT OF CYRSTALLIZATION

Shining in winter moonlight --
the molecules of our breath
stretch across the glass
reaching for space in which
to give up their small bits of heat
in an exquisite geometry of avoidance.

Opening my eyes at sunrise I watch as---
released by warmth, the molecules
retreat, regroup, converge, confront, cohere –
each crystal branch becomes a liquid sphere.

MARCH COMES IN ----

A slashing storm today,
wind rushing overhead like a freight train,
cedars shimmying crazily.
Rachmaninoff is singing in my ear
of passion, struggle and triumph

Elizabeth King

I AM

    I am – composed mostly of empty space with a pinch of pretty ordinary chemicals: carbon, hydrogen, oxygen, nitrogen silica, calcium, magnesium – etc... nothing very exotic or expensive – the stuff you find lying around almost anywhere in any kind of life form on the planet. The almost entirely empty space, which I am accustomed to call "me," is thinly populated with subatomic particles grouped (why? how?) into atoms stuck together into molecules which are stuck together into cells that assemble themselves into a variety of living tissues which somehow miraculously end up in the right places. For example, we grow eyelashes on our eyelids and fingernails on our fingers pretty reliably. How do you suppose the cells know how to do that?

    All of this body stuff is continually breaking down and building itself up again using huge amounts of energy, which we somehow manage to manufacture out of equally mysterious foodstuffs. We can name the forces that drive the process and hold all these particles together, and we have some knowledge of how these forces can be expected to behave (that's medicine!), but beyond the names we give them, we really don't know much about them. The biggest unanswered question is, Why??

    Why do these particles like to hang out together and keep regrouping into the same configurations? (Well, not quite the same – the skin develops wrinkles and the hair turns white). The configurations that I call "Bonnie" or "Marge" or "Bob" or "Vince" are consistent enough so that we recognize each other from week to week and even from year to year – decade to decade. If that isn't amazing, I don't know what is!

    The conclusion I draw from all this is that "I am" essentially an idea – a particular arrangement like a car or a painting or a building – with the difference that the arrangement that is "me" keeps renewing and perpetuating itself driven by forces that I do not understand. I wonder if this isn't a way of understanding immortality? After all, what is the life span of an idea?

    I am.......... A mystery......... And so are you.

Elizabeth King

GRANDMOTHERS

Although I had both grandmothers living near us and saw them often, my close "grandmother" relationship was with my great-aunt Katherine whom I often used to visit after school. She has been in my mind especially of late because my own 7-year old grandchild is in love with hand sewing, a process that I learned to love during those long afternoons in the upstairs room where "Tanting" (little aunt), being the maiden-aunt-in-residence, did the family sewing. Lilly, like my own small-child self, loves sewing doll clothes. Lilly sews for her Barbies. I sewed for a collection of small sawdust-stuffed animals that Tanting had brought with her all the way from Germany.

Tanting never married because as a young woman she had had a double mastectomy for cancer – probably without an anesthetic, and the resulting disfigurement permanently disqualified her for marriage, as was the mindset of the times. She lived with my grandfather - her brother and best childhood friend and his family which was an easy walk from my elementary school and my home. As young people in Friesland, which is now Germany, they were born into the Danish occupation. My grandfather kept a journal about that occupation and the war that ended it. The family left Germany to escape the impending Franco-Prussian war. They had seen enough of war and the waste and destruction that went with it, not to mention the sacrifice of another generation of young men.

As young people, Katherine and her brother Wilhelm lived for the yearly advent of a travelling theater company where they volunteered for everything that could possibly need doing in exchange for access to the performances and friendships with the actors and producers. In another destiny, Tanting would have joined the troupe and designed and created costumes and sets – but her family was too respectable to consider that possibility – and theater was too frivolous to be considered as a vocation for Wilhelm. I have old photographs as well as my grandfather's journals telling the story of that early enthusiasm which has surfaced again here and there in my children and grandchildren.

Elizabeth King

Tanting's cancer never troubled her again, and she lived to see me married. Her family did not consider her enough of a personage, though, for me to be notified of her death or invited to participate in the ceremonies that marked her passing. I was living in another part of the country. To me she is still a living presence and always will be.

MIGRATION

>Flung into the sky, a thousand wings flicker
>dipping and turning as one,
>now black against the horizon,
>now sliver-thin, almost invisible,
>held together by signals too subtle for my eyes –
>No! wait! A few dozen are left behind!
>Missed the cue, fallen away from the flock
>but only for a moment, the breach is healed,
>magically, like torn lace mending by a miracle,
>Like children playing "crack the whip,"
>they wheel again. It is a game of wits --
>no bodily cord ties these together,
>but something stronger. I feel it in myself.
>Something in my bloodstream feels that pull.
>I am sucked up into the air to follow that flock
>all the way to Mexico or Honduras
>or wherever it is they are going

Elizabeth King

THE LEONIDS

Sitting on my doorstep, my own small feline
warmly in my lap, looking for a meteor shower.
Not a meteor in sight – we must be too early –
but a splendid night for stargazing , the air as clear
as it will ever be, and much more sky
available now that the leaves are off of the trees.
There are Betelgeuse and Rigel in the constellation of Orion,
Aldeberan in Taurus, and Sirius in Canis Major,
Procyon in Canis Minor, and Pollux in the constellation
of Gemini, As we watch, the sky begins
to cloud over. Pretty nippy out here –
cat and I go back inside, appreciating
the warmth of the kitchen. An Amaryllis bud
is poking up out of a dry pot, unbidden,
demanding to be watered and fed. Back
to small earthly tasks. The cosmos will take care of itself.

SOLICE

At the extreme farthest fling
Into dark and coldness and death,
we are most kindly and gently
caught, and held and turned
back toward the source
of warmth and light and life ---
That fiercely blazing furnace
that would scorch us into
nothingness ----except we are
once more most kindly and gently
caught and held and turned ------

Dottie Moody

Dottie Moody is a Maine native. She has a Master of Library Science and a Master of Divinity. Her work has been primarily clerical. Learning has always been her greatest interest. Write On, a local writing group, is responsible for Dottie fulfilling her lifelong desire to write. She's just begun writing poetry. She wants to fill her senior years with reading, writing and learning.

Dottie Moody

WRITE ON
dedicated to Bonnie Wheeler

Wednesday afternoon at 1:00
is my church
is my cathedral

Here the written word is sacred
Each one strives
to carve their own words
on the tablet of truth

No one is judged
All are esteemed

There is no hush
There is
reading
laughing
caring
encouragement

In valuing the written word
we also value each other

Dottie Moody

SACRED SPACE

Poetry is now my church
Emily Dickinson said it so well
It's not a building you visit

The chapel is within
and
around us

Just listen
How often do we listen to nature?
How often do we listen
to the voice within?

Poetry allows us to linger
where others have worshiped
Poetry can transport us
to a holy place

Dottie Moody

SERMONS OR POETRY?

I have a
Master of Divinity
I might deliver
a sermon or two a week

Do I want to write
sermons
often
soon forgotten

When I can write poetry
which can live on
for those
who love language as I do

I'm not disparaging
those sermons
I am just listening to
my inner truth

I love the rocks and rills
of poetry
I love words
of all varieties

To play with words
until they reveal
what they have to say
This is my joy

Dottie Moody

HE'S BEAUTIFUL
dedicated to Stanley Kunitz

I want to live to be as old as he.
Look at his picture!

No more worries
about beauty or handsomeness
all you see is age

Over ninety is my goal
with mind intact
and slow motion possible

To still create
words
beauty
flowers

There is beauty
in advanced old age
not physical beauty
spiritual beauty

You've heard so much
You've seen so much
You've lived so much

God grant you other ears
to hear your wisdom

God grant you comfort
in physical infirmities

For just a little longer

Dottie Moody

FOR THIS ONE DAY

For this one day
I choose to let go
of fear

Fear will not
allow me
to have a good day

For this one day
I choose to let go
of unforgiveness
and its negativity

For this one day
I am going to
appreciate the sunshine
stay busy
love everyone

I am not going to
borrow trouble
from tomorrow

This is my choice
for today

Dottie Moody

PEACE

If your thoughts are
getting dark and ugly
don't go there

There are alternatives
you are turning away
from the light

Light keeps the earth turning
Light keeps us free
from all the negative emotions
that want to tear us down

If something
is making you angry
don't follow its trail

Your mind has the power
to calm those thoughts down
It's a choice

Pick the way that
won't add fuel to the fire

Pick the way that
will lead you
to brighter days

It's our choice
anger
or peace

Choose peace

Dottie Moody

KITTIE

Writing poetry
with a cat on my lap

Guess who's not getting
enough attention,
looks imploringly up at me?

Now I ask you Kittie
which is more important
my poem
or
your need for attention?

Do I ever bother you
when you are working away?
What you don't work?
What do you do?

I rest my case
you can have my attention
as soon as you become
more productive.

Dottie Moody

TO INDIA

Flying across the Pacific
first to London
New Delhi's fog lifts
on to India

First night spent
in a hotel
complete with attendants
sleeping on the floor
outside the rooms

In the morning
the train station
Waiting on hard seats
to go to Kota in Rajasthan

the restroom a choice of
two kinds of toilets
neither clean

An ancient looking train
we are among the fortunate
second class ticket holders

we have seats
even opportunity
for some to stretch out
and rest

In Kota
another new experience
an auto rickshaw

in a blur,
transporting us to
Emmanuel Ministries

The dorm
at last
something familiar

Dottie Moody

WHAT HAVE I DONE?

A five year old walking a two year old
up the street
to the grocery store

Returning I crossed the street
Two year old sister
did not follow

I coaxed her to cross
There are no cars coming
hurry

When she decided to comply
there was a car coming
Blood on the grill
Blood on sister's head

What have I done?
Driver takes sister to the hospital
I go home
and tell Daddy

Daddy, no shoes on,
runs to the police station
to find his baby

LOST PICTURES

Mike and Tommy
sitting on folding chairs
at the end of the empty rental truck
at my new apartment

Mom
sleeping on her side
with her hands extended
folded as if in prayer

Two piles of driftwood
debarked, piled high
on Popham Beach
thick maritime ropes attached

Blurry pictures of mom
surreptitiously taken
by Mike
during her last hospital stay
Mom looking lost and unhappy

Lois sitting on the earth
at Mom's grave
planting flowers
with the twins

Have I remembered them all?
I want to remember
With these words
I'll always remember

Dottie Moody

TIME

Maybe it is appropriate
this shortening of tasks I do

Instead of writing prose
I write poems

Instead of reading books
I read poems

As my remaining years shorten
Brevity creeps into
my creative efforts

When I'm gone

Perhaps it will be a poem
left unread
not a book

Perhaps it will be a poem
unwritten
not a story

Subtle these changes
they are not to be overlooked

As in the beginning
life was opening up
Now its petals are folding

Wendall Kinney

Wendall is a fifth generation Maine native who was born "Down East" in the county of Washington and the town of Danforth. He grew up on a dairy farm in Central Maine. He is a graduate of The Aroostook Central Institute and has a bachelor's degree from Norwich University. He is a US Army veteran having served in Japan and Korea. He and his wife Mona have two grown children. He is retired from The Portsmouth Naval Shipyard in Kittery, Maine and lives in Brunswick.

Wendall has been writing poetry and prose since 1990. His book of short stories, "Over Home and Other Kitchen Table Tales," is based on family history.

He has a new CD of Maine humor entitled *The Bull and I*.

Wendall Kinney

1941 OLDSMOBILE

It was glossy green, sleek, and trim. The white walls sparkled in the late afternoon sun and caught my eye like a magnet as I stepped from my father's truck in the used car lot. We walked toward my first car. A man in a wide flowered tie, suspenders, and a striped shirt, stepped from a small building at the edge of the lot, blew smoke he had sucked from a big cigar, and walked toward us.

Had I known then what I later found out, I might have gotten back into Dad's truck and left. Shoulda, woulda, coulda!

Guess that's neither here nor there now.

He tipped his felt hat and extended a beefy hand to my father and ignored me since I was a mere teen at the time. "Good afternoon, I'm George Casey," he said in a deep rumbling voice. My dad shook his hand.

"My son is looking for his first car and has his eye on that Oldsmobile."

"Well I'll say this for him, he has good taste," George responded and turned to acknowledge me. "That's the best car on the lot, and I can let you have it for two hundred dollars."

"That's a little more than we planned to pay," Dad said. "Come on, son, we'll go and see about that little coupe at Mountain's Ford. That might be a better buy."

"Now hold on. That ain't my final price. You guys look like good folks. I'll let you have it for one seventy five."

"We'll have to try it out," Dad said.

We bought it for one hundred sixty eight dollars, and I drove it towards home, proud as a peacock. My euphoria lasted until I started down the hill just beyond Hall's seed farm. I applied the brakes to slow the downhill momentum. They worked fine at first and then began to fade. I pumped them as I had been taught. By the time I got to the bottom of that hill, my foot was pushing the pedal to the floor boards. I managed to get it home without going in the ditch by using the gears as brakes.

I pulled into the yard as Dad was just getting out of his truck. "How did it go, son?" he asked, and I told him. He would have hit the roof had we not been outside. As it was, he called George Casey several very bad names. "Come on," he said and slid in behind the wheel of the Olds.

"Well, now, I can't be held responsible for everything that might be wrong with these old cars," George said shaking his head in mock dismay. "Once you leave the lot – it's yours."

I had that car for a little over a year. Besides the master brake cylinder that had to be replaced, the shocks were gone, and it would rock for hours after going over a bump. The piston rings were so bad the combustion pressurized the crank case and blew oil out the fill pipe.

My last adventure with it was a trip from Mars Hill to Danforth one November night with a car load of high school friends. Besides being stopped by a State Trooper for defective equipment (tail light), that old Oldsmobile ran out of oil and quit about midnight on the way back home twenty miles from nowhere. We were lucky enough to get a ride in the back of a farmer's truck into Mars Hill.

Dad took me back to retrieve my first car the next morning. We got it home, but the old Olds died for good shortly thereafter.

That 1941 Oldsmobile taught me at least three of life's lessons:
1. Just because it looks good doesn't mean it is – or beauty is only skin deep.
2. Buyer beware – especially when buying a used car.
3. Never trust a salesman with a flowered tie and a striped shirt – especially if he's smoking a big cigar.

Come to think of it – that car was worth the money after all.

Wendall Kinney

DUNBAR B & B

It sits in what was once a field but is now a forest of mixed pine and maple. It was once the center of evil in a small Massachusetts town. The outside is painted a light tan, and the trim and shutters reflect magenta. The inside is warm and well lit with decorative lamps and chandeliers. The appearance had always given me a sense of peace and comfort when I had stopped here on my way to Boston.

I had spent a full day in my home office in Wiscasset, Maine before driving to Salem and was ready for a soft bed and good night's rest.

I was greeted on my arrival, not by Mrs. Dunbar the proprietress, but by a tall lady dressed as if she were going to a costume ball. Her hair was done up under a black cap pinned to the back of her head, her blouse was black with long sleeves, and her skirt reached the floor.

"Welcome, welcome, to Dunbar. I'm Goodwife Cory, the night clerk." she said and gestured to a little girl by her side that I would guess was about five years old. "This is Dorcas Good. You will meet her mother later. The little girl curtsied and smiled shyly from behind Mrs. Cory's long skirt.

Mrs. Cory jotted down my name in a ledger. "You're lucky, for you have the last room tonight. Our rooms are all full," she continued and laughed with a high pitched chuckle.

"Where is Mrs. Dunbar?" I asked and placed my overnight bag on the floor near the desk.

"Oh, she and Mr. Dunbar have gone to Gloucester for the night. They do that every year on this night. She said you would be coming and so here you are. You have your regular room at the top of the stairs. As soon as you put your bags away why don't you join the other guests in the lounge for a harvest drink?" she said and handed me a key. I thought I heard her say, "Thou shall be our witness", but when I turned to make sure, she was gone.

Upon entering the lounge a few minutes later I was greeted by a young woman. She was dressed in a colonial-like garb as had been Mrs. Cory. There was one exception – around her neck was what looked very much like a piece of rope.

"I'm Sarah," she said "Sarah Good, I think you have already met my daughter."

She took my arm and introduced me to the others in the room. "This is Goodwife Nurse and here is Goodwife Dustin and here we have Goody Osborne." They all curtsied respectfully. "I hear you are to be our witness," Goodwife Dustin said.

I asked what that meant but was ignored while a drink which tasted like pumpkin and apple cider was pressed into my hand by Goody Osborne.

"Is there a Mister Osborne?" I asked her, for I noticed there were no other men in the room.

"Oh, there was once but he has been gone a long time," she said and then continued, "You're wondering why there are no other men in the room. They are all down there." She gestured toward the basement, or so I thought at the time.

Mrs. Good came in with a tray of donuts. "I see you have met everyone," she said as she placed the tray on the coffee table. I took another drink from my glass and felt a warm glow begin to spread from my stomach. "There must be something more in this glass than pumpkin juice," I thought as my head began to swim just a little.

I sat down in a comfortable chair as my head continued to spin and watched abstractly as Mrs. Osborne and Mrs. Dustin wheeled a long desk to one side of the room. On the desk rested a large black book. To this desk went the Mrs. Cory, Good, Osborne, Dustin and Nurse. They sat down behind it. The little girl Dorcas was nowhere to be seen.

"Indian John, bring forth the accused Reverend Parris," said Mrs. Cory.

A West Indian-looking black man entered leading a tall stork-like man in a ragged wool suit. There were holes in the elbows and knees. His shirt was a dirty-white as was his face as he looked through red rimmed eyes.

"Reverend Parris, you are accused of complacency in the murder of Sarah Good in that you did nothing to stop the hysteria brought forth by your daughter and your slave Tibuta. That hysteria resulted in the hanging of Goody Good. How do you plead?"

Wendall Kinney

"I am guilty. I have suffered in Hell for all these many years, and whatever you do here tonight cannot be worse than that."

"What say you each," the tribunal was polled.

"Forgive him" was the verdict.

"Bring forth John Hawthorne, Jonathan Cowin, James Russell, Isaac Addington, Major Samuel Appleton, Captain Samuel Sewall, and Deputy Governor Thomas Danforth."

The seven accused were brought before the bench by Indian Joe.

"You are each accused of premeditated murder in the deaths of Sarah Good, Sarah Osborne, Sarah Dustin, Martha Cory and Rebecca Nurse. How do you plead?"

The man called Deputy Governor Danforth stepped forward. He was a sorry sight. His once fashionable, I suppose, dress was now in rags. His face was soot-covered as well as his hands and hose. "I speak for us all. We were the magistrates, charged with judging the truth in the claims of witchcraft. We found the girls, Elizabeth Parris, Abigail Williams, and the rest to truly be possessed by Satan. And we also found that the before mentioned Goodwives were instruments of Satan – witches. We still hold that to be true after all these years as Satan's guests in hell."

"What say you each?" the tribunal was again polled.

"Send them back to Hell," was the verdict.

"Bring forth the last accused, Indian John."

Giles Cory was led into the room by the West Indian.

"You are charged with lying and sending your wife to the gallows. How do you plead?"

"For God's sake Martha, help me," he begged, seeing his wife behind the bench. "I have suffered all these many years for what I said that day at the trial."

"I will help you as you helped me," she said. "You testified thusly -

"The evidence of Giles Choree testifieth & saith that Last satturday in the Evening. sitting by the fire my wife asked me to go to bed. I told I would go to prayr. & when I went to prayer I could nott utter my desires w'th any sense, not open my mouth to speake My wife did perceive itt & came towards. me & said she was coming to me. After this in alittle space I did according to my measure attend the duty.

Wendall Kinney

Sometime last weake I fetcht an ox well out the woods, about noone, & he laying down in the yard I went to raise him to yoake him butt he could not rise butt dragd his hinder parts as if he had been hiptshott, butt after did rise.

I had a Catt somtimes last weeke strangly taken on the suddain & did make me think she would have died presently, #[butt] my wife bid me knock her in the head. butt I did not. & since she is well. Another time going to duties I was interrupted for aspace, butt aftterward I was helpt according to my poore measure.

My wife hath ben wont to sitt up after I went to bed, & I have perceived her to kneel down to the harth. as if she were at prayr, but heard nothing.
March: 24'th 1691/2" *

"What say you each," the tribunal was polled.
"Send him back to hell for evermore."

I awoke the next morning in my customary room with a head as big as a pumpkin. I showered and shaved, dressed and went down for breakfast. To my surprise, I was greeted by Mrs. Dunbar. "Did you sleep well?" She asked. "I thought you and Mr. Dunbar were in Gloucester." I said.

"Oh, no, what ever gave you an idea like that?"

*Essex county Archives, Salem – Witchcraft – Vol 1, page 13

Oh, My Aching Back

"Oh, my aching back" is a commonly used expression of dissatisfaction with an event or situation. It may or may not be related to an actual aching back. Back being the posterior of the human anatomy. That is, the area of the human anatomy in the rear of the abdomen. The abdomen is that part of the human anatomy immediately below the chest and above the pelvis. The Chest being that part of the anatomy commonly referred to in medical circles as the thorax and is just below the neck. The neck being the part of the anatomy just below the head and is often another place that is painful as in "Oh, what a pain in the neck he is." The neck contains the larynx or voice box and is located below the cranium which contains the brain, and we all know it is responsible for the aching back and the pain in the neck

Gladys Szabo

Gladys was born in Jamaica, New York, moved to Connecticut at the age of one, and then to Maine in 2000. She has two children, Robert and Dawn, and four granddaughters.

While raising her family, Gladys was active in Boy Scouts and Girl Scouts, and continues with Girl Scouting as a leader and a Neighborhood Team member going on her 27th year.

Working for Independence Association was an important part of her life since she moved to Maine. It was more than just a job. She made several very close personal relationships with people, some of whom remain in her life as extended family.

The greatest joys in Gladys's life are her family, friends, pets, and meeting new people. These along with her passion for animals, crafts, and volunteering, are the focus for most of her writings.

Writing has always been a hobby for Gladys and was the reason she joined the "Write On! group" in 2009. Since becoming a member, she has expanded her creativity and writing techniques, and is also working on her memoirs.

Gladys Szabo

NEW FAMILY MEMBER

I adopted Sunny, my cat, one year ago, but then decided I wanted a dog also, so I adopted Noel.

"Hey I think we need to have a chat." Sunny implies.
"Not Me!"
"Why Not?"
"I am not sure about you."
"Why not?"
"You are always sneaking around me sniffing, and you look scary."
"I just want to get to know you."
"Why do you need to know me? Can't you just leave me alone and go your own way?"
"Well, I was lonely and like having you here. We can be good pals, stick together."
"Well, maybe, but it is going to take time-so take it slowly."
"Ok, well, thanks for letting me get a little closer for now."

Gladys Szabo

THE BLIZZARD OF 1977

The year was "77". Snow was predicted. By ten A.M. white fluffy snowflakes were lightly falling. Schools let out at noon. Work places shut down. My husband was home before the school kids. My daughter, Dawn, was home from Middle School by one. She appeared like an Eskimo in a snow globe as she trudged up the driveway after walking a half mile from the bus stop.

The CB radio truckers were chatting about road and traffic conditions. The police scanner was not very active. My son, Rob, was usually home from High School by two. As the time approached 2:30, I called neighbors to inquire if any of their kids had arrived home. They were worried. They told me there was no sign of the bus, and the main roads were not looking very good. Truckers informed us of blinding snow on Highway I84, the route the school buses traveled. The scanner started getting busier.

"Traffic on I84 is slowing down to a crawl!"

We now knew the buses would be late. It was getting close to four o'clock. Scary news on scanner!

"We cannot locate bus 52. We have no communication. It is the only bus without a radio!"

My son's bus!!! I made a frantic call to the truckers, "Can anyone see a yellow school bus on I84? " Quick responses came. No one had seen the bus, but they would be on the lookout for it. I nervously called the police station, "I am wondering what you are doing to locate bus 52?"

"We are in contact with them. They are in traffic on I84!"

"No, you're not. I have a scanner and know you can't locate them!"

Trying to reassure me, the officer responded, "We have snowmobiles scanning the highway searching for the bus!"

Listening to the scanner was NOT reassuring!! We heard, "No sight of a bus. Snow is blinding and it's difficult to see more than a few feet."

My body ached with fear as I observed drifts forming mountains in our driveway and against the doors. Panic struck as I felt trapped while my son was stuck on a bus no one could find. Having our family separated during a storm was dreadful.

Gladys Szabo

    Listening to truckers and police still not able to sight the bus was horrifying! Frantically, friends and neighbors were sharing whatever news they could obtain. Phones ringing, calls to the police, all fearing the unknown outcome!

    Now, nearly four hours after our children should have been home, darkness was making the situation significantly scarier. My stomach was in knots. Frightening thoughts were raging. I worried not only about my son but all the kids on that cold bus. Were they as scared as we were?

    Suddenly the CB lights were blinking wildly. I heard an excited trucker, "I see the bus! They are ahead of us stopped in traffic. They are located on the hill heading down to the Middlebury exit!" Frantically I notified the police of the bus's location.

    Over an hour later the scanner reported, "We have reached the bus by snowmobile. The kids are fine and warm. They are partying with a Hostess truck driver who is generously sharing his goods with them! Police cruisers will meet the bus at the highway exit and assure all get home safely!"

    Finally at seven o'clock, another announcement came across the scanner. "The bus is exiting off the highway! Police officer, Danny Gardiner is taking over the bus, relieving a much shaken bus driver." The kids were dropped off as close to their homes as possible.

The darkness, blinding snow, and drifts several feet high, made the walk home impossible for most of the neighborhood kids. Friends living at the entrance to our development kindly offered to keep everyone at their house for the night till they could safely get home sometime the next day.

    We were thrilled that Rob and all the others were safe and warm for the night, but I wasn't totally relieved until he walked through the door at ten the next morning rambling excitedly about his "fun" adventure - his NOT MINE!

Gladys Szabo

A TRIBUTE TO "MY DADS"

    Albert, my biological dad, educated me regarding the true values of life. He was a living example. Rather than using words, he taught me honesty, kindness, to be helpful, and most of all, loving and accepting of all people. My dad's radiant smile and sense of humor could transform a room of somber people into laughter and joy. His priorities were family, friends, and community. I watched with anticipation when as a volunteer fireman, he braved burning buildings, flames lighting the night's dark sky, and gas tanks exploding. I cried with relief knowing he was safe as he emerged from the rubble covered in ashes.

    Even though I was his only child, I would accompany my dad when he was setting up playgrounds in the city, or coaching a little league team. He enthusiastically attended every event in which I took part. We were inseparable.

    Our nightly trips for ice cream, or snuggling in the warmed blankets he wrapped me in as I climbed into my cold bed, are just two of many special memories I hold in my heart. I was his side kick and helper no matter what task he tackled. Most important to me were his loving heart and warm hugs, as he would embrace me in his strong arms.

    At the age of forty four, my dad suddenly died of a heart attack. I was fourteen and devastated!

    Several years after my dad's death, my mom married Roland. He became a "dad" rather than a stepdad in every sense of the word. He never tried to replace my dad. His respect for my feelings was touching. We laughed and cried through life's ups and downs.

    He patiently taught me to drive. He beamed as "my dad" when I graduated High School, and the day I married he walked me down the aisle weeping with emotion.

    Like my "dad", his actions spoke louder than words and taught me to respect everyone, including myself. Even though I was a teenager when he came into my life, we shared wonderful times and bonded in a very special relationship. He was great at working out "teenage issues" between my mom and me. He loved introducing me as "his daughter!"

    At age thirty six, married and mother of two children, I was legally adopted by Pop-Pop (as we called him). He wanted us to be his legal family. As we walked out of the court room you'd have thought he won the lottery. He excitedly told anyone and everyone, "This is my daughter and grandchildren!"

I am truly blessed to have had two extraordinary dads in my life. I am the person I am today because of their loving guidance and still striving to live up to their ideals.

MORNING SERENTIY

Morning sun
Sharing its brilliancy
Over my bed.
Soothing my body
With its warmth.
Sunny, My cat,
Snuggling,
Sharing butterfly kisses
Upon my face.
Noel, My dog
Lodged tight
Against my curved knees.
The morning quietness
Bestows a peacefulness
Unlike most mornings
My eyes close
Delighting in the serenity
Of the moment
Thanking God
For this rare moment in time!

Gladys Szabo

THE ACCIDENTAL HOOKER

I headed to Mere Point Marina to chaperone my granddaughter's 7th grade field trip. The buses unloaded. No granddaughter. I inquired about Monica's whereabouts and was told she would arrive with the second group.

Gray, milky clouds covered the sky as the trees waltzed in the whipping wind. Waves were lurching like a roller coaster as the docks jerked like riders on the coaster. The scent of the salt air brought vivid memories of days gone by. Walk those docks? Do I dare?

"Everyone out to your stations on the docks!" announced the teacher.

Shuddering as I anxiously approached the docks, I prayed I wouldn't plummet into the water! I was totally intimidated by charging youngsters. My body quivered as if walking a tight rope. I tried to retain my balance, but it was like walking on ice. My thought was to keep moving and look straight ahead as the frigid water lashed the docks. When I reached the center of the docks, I planted my feet and wasn't moving another step!

As I searched the groups, I located a friend, and we apprehensively ventured back to stable ground. Reaching land, I became intrigued with a crane operator. He appeared seaworthy, operating the crane like a pro. He lowered a cable with a grungy hook attached and almost caught the rusty chain of an immense anchor. I wondered if he would hook it with the crane. Unable to do so, he climbed down to hook it manually.

"I thought you would hook it with the crane!" I commented

"I used to in my younger days, no more. I'm about 2 inches short of the chain. Would you mind hooking it as I lower it?"

"Not a problem."

As he lowered the hook, I attached it to the anchor, making sure it was secure. I took several steps back as it went up swinging and swaying, and he lowered it into a boat.

The next thing I knew I was wearing filthy gloves and performing this job for the next hour!

Several teachers commented with laughter on my new job.

My granddaughter finally arrived. We tackled the docks together. I was now feeling more confident with my granddaughter as my anchor.

Gladys Szabo

LOVE AT FIRST SIGHT

Do I believe
In love at first sight?
It happened to me
One magical night.

I entered a party
And smiles were exchanged.
All of a sudden
I felt a bit strange.

My heart was beating
Like a snare drum.
My stomach had the jitters
My legs went all numb.

I searched for him
As he graciously mingled.
Too shy to approach
Having just become single.

The evening was ending
Without having met
Chances were gone
Was my first bet.

To my surprise
A second chance came along.
He asked me to dance
To a slow easy song.

I never did notice
That very first night
He never did let me
Out of his sight.

Gladys Szabo

LOVING MEMORIES OF AUNT ETHEL

A Guardian Angel now in Heaven
I still feel the warmth of your presence
Whenever I needed to bend your ear
You listened, then shared what I needed to hear

Helping me to always see
Life as it is or how it could be
Never judging, just offering advice
A soft shoulder to lean on, Oh so nice

An Aunt by marriage, my closest friend
You spoke truthfully till the end
Telling me exactly what was on your mind
Not always what I wanted to find

Yet, never an angry word we shared
Honesty and fairness not to be compared
You will always be in my heart
In the sky, the brightest part

When I close my eyes, I see your face
In quiet times, I feel your grace
So many times, you eased my strife
Still today, you influence my life.

Every day I am so thankful
To have had you as my Guardian Angel
Heartfelt thanks with all my Love
First on Earth, and now Above

Gladys Szabo

MOTHER'S DAY REFLECTIONS

Reflecting back on Mother's Day
Is that why my hair is grey?
My son was born August twenty sixth, nineteen sixty four.
My life from that day forth was never a bore!
My daughter arrived December fourth, nineteen sixty seven.
A son and daughter, I was in heaven.
Occasional pains but abundance of joys.
House strewn with books and toys
Sometimes I wish I could go back.
Life moves too quickly, that's a fact.
They grew too fast.
I am aghast!
Flourishing adults lives of their own.
Their needs for me have far out grown.
My son free falls out of a plane.
Why this? I can't explain.
My daughter is a devoted Mom.
So now a "Nanny" I've become.

THE NEST

My eyes were draw to the sky as a bird, toting a branch larger than he, appeared above me. The bird's image against the cloudless sky, gliding with superlative wing span, was a magnificent sight. He dipped back and forth with the wind, determined not to lose his treasure. This reoccurring sight continued for days until his nest was completed, resting upon a plank between the power poles.

The nest was majestic compared to the size of the bird. Day after day, he sat on the pole or the lines, letting neither rain nor wind distract his watch over his nest. In time, eggs were hatched, and Mother bird appeared, sitting on the edge of the nest feeding the babies, while Father continued his watch.

This family continues to return every year in spite of their home having been destroyed by storms several times. This to me is a wonder of nature

Adelaide Guernelli

Adelaide was born in Italy. She received a B.A. and M.A. degree in Humanities and Education at the University of Puerto Rico and her Ph. D at NYU.

Adelaide is the author of *Me Visto de Corazon*, a book of poetry; a collaborator in various textbooks and has written literary criticism in *El Mundo, Manhattan Mind, La Torre,* and other newspapers in Puerto Rico, New York, Italy, and Mexico. She is a member of several learned societies and has lectured in universities.

Adelaide lives in Brunswick, near family, and wishes to expand her writings in English so her grandchildren will remember her fully.

Adelaide Guernelli

THANKSGIVING DAY

Today, the night of life wakes up
on this side of the world
where millions of people live and,
though they are extremely different
they are united…at least today,
to make their diversity, a unity of gladness
to celebrate the humanized equality,
in the language of the dining table
with a superlative length of Life.
All seem to be tying their different roots in one country,
while invoking the grace
with the thousand names of God.

A SONG I HEARD IN MAINE

I heard it one day in Maine.
It was a song that said,
"You are going to catch a cold
from the ice inside your soul."

Poets try to learn how the ocean works.
Its depth is very important they feel,
as it creates the souls
of all poets on Earth.

LIFE AND DEATH

Life can be a dream.
Life can teach us to dance.
Life can be books full of important ideas.
Life can be a protector of our bodies.
And…
Life can be the way we prepare for death,
completing the Circle of Living.

Adelaide Guernelli

ONLY ONE AT A TIME

One day at a time,
They say that we die,
Or it might just be a way
Of hugging the sky.
One day you're born from somebody,
Or maybe, it's you yourself
Who comes to this world,
Slowly allowing that he or she
Play the role of being parents
Predecided by God.

One day at a time,
Life vanishes well,
In a foaming experience
Of breathing the days.
One day at a time, only one day…!
All what makes you a person
Becomes one with the earth,
And just with the soil and,
The thoughts that you were,
Fly deep inside, very strangely diluted
In the pores of time.

But, before it happens, God saves us the soul
That was hidden so tightly, in the fabric of Time…
That nobody could see, in the game that…
Is…just LIFE.!

Ann Robinson

Ann was born in California and grew up in northern Ohio. She graduated from the University of Akron and embarked on a teaching career in the U.S., indulging her wanderlust in Ohio, Florida, New Mexico and Texas. While in Texas she discovered the amazing prospects of teaching overseas with the American Military and immediately applied. She spent the next 23 years teaching Mathematics and Biology to military dependents in Germany and South Korea while exploring the world outside of the U.S. In 2010 she retired to Brunswick, Maine, where she now lives on the edge of the Commons with her golden retriever, Darcy.

In Brunswick she discovered the Write-On Group and switched from solving equations to solving plot lines. She is compelled to write stories about her golden retriever who insists on having a voice. She also delves into science fiction and fantasy, and is drawn to tales with a twist, or with the badly behaved receiving their comeuppance.

Ann Robinson

A TAIL OF TWO PARENTS

My dad had a way with dogs. They worshipped him. Put a dog in the same room and the dog would gravitate to him in a flash. At my dad's funeral a hunting buddy told a story about my dad and dogs. Years ago, another buddy had had a young, very large, and very untrained black lab who was wild and crazy, the canine form of ADHD. The dog was never still and never obedient. In a room with people he was a hurricane, constantly moving, no object or body part safe from bouncing paws, slobbering tongue, or pounding tail. His owner kept him locked away when visitors were present.

There was one time though when several of the buddies were gathered at the owner's house telling tales and drinking beer when Wild Thing got loose. As the owner grabbed empty air, the dog scanned the room and made straight for my dad, charging past the five other men and tables laden with meat and cheese. He jumped in my dad's lap and sat there calmly for the next hour looking out at the room as if to say: "Pay attention. This is how it's supposed to be. "

Dogs would always find my dad. My mother? Not so much. We always had dogs when I was growing up, but they were my dad's dogs, not my mother's. And mostly not mine, although I did get a little action now and then, but never my mother. She avoided them and they her. She was busy raising me, teaching English, grading papers, cleaning house, and cooking. There was just no time for dogs. Once, after I had left home, she expressed her frustration with my dad and his dogs. They weren't people, after all. Molly, his German Shorthair Pointer, was about to have pups, and my dad had spent the entire night in the basement with her. My mother could not believe it. "Do you know what your Father did? I will never understand him. It's a dog for Pete's sake." I did not let on that I understood.

Ann Robinson

Then my Dad died. They had retired to Corpus Christi, TX some years before and built a house out on Padre Island when it was still remote and sparsely populated. Katie, my dad's last dog, was getting old, so we suggested to my mother that she consider getting a puppy. I had a golden retriever, and she decided she was willing to look at a litter but not convinced she wanted one. There was a good breeder in Houston from whom I had gotten my dog, and she happened to have a litter ready to go, so we drove to Houston. There were two pups left, and when my mother saw them it was over. An army could not have kept her from those pups. She instantly bonded with the pup she picked up and named her Samantha, Sam for short. And of course it was her dog. My Dad was not there, and no one else was in the house. Years later when Sam the dog was getting older, she brought up that previous conversation and confessed that she now completely understood my dad and his dogs.

DOGGONE

    Today was the third day of the Change, and the Chihuahua holding my leash was becoming tiresome. This morning we did ten walks before noon. The collar was again too tight and no amount of pointing, gesturing, or whining affected him. He is a feisty little thing, and loving his new role. He sat and patiently watched my attempts at communication, then, with a snort, headed again for the door. I tried to resist. I figured if I just sat in a chair and refused to get up, what could he do? He was a Chihuahua after all. Well, let me tell you, that didn't work. He went to the door, barked twice, and within seconds, I was confronted by a St Bernard, two Great Danes, a Burmese Mountain Dog, and a Standard Poodle, all standing in a semi-circle in front of my chair. The Big Dogs. I was in trouble. Each of the dogs took a bite on my 10 foot leash, and together they pulled until the choke collar around my neck tightened to the point that I could not breathe, and I gave up. Now when the Chihuahua heads for the door, I just go.
    None of us in the town have been able to remove either the collar or the leash. When our hands get close they are repelled like two magnets of the same polarity but much, much stronger. We have all tried with our hands and with tools. Nothing works. The dogs just sit and watch. A few howl. Some snort. Nor have any of us been able to resist. The Big Dogs arrive, and we can't compete. Those who resist are bullied into submission. It is difficult to deny a St. Bernard sitting on your chest. One man who collects guns attempted a coup. He was startled to discover in the act of shooting at the Big Dogs that his gun would not fire. None of his guns would fire. The dogs sat patiently waiting for him to give up. And of course he did. What else could he do?
    I did not have a dog before the Change. Why I now have a Chihuahua is beyond me. My neighbor is an older lady with a golden retriever. Sometimes the Chihuahua and the Golden walk us together growling, whining, barking at each other in turn. They lead, we follow. Once in a while, they turn to look at us and howl together before moving on.

None of us can speak. We have the ability only to growl, whine, yip, and snarl. Several people in the town know sign language and are teaching the rest of us whenever we can meet up on walks or at the dog park, so at least we can still communicate as humans.

We are allowed to eat once a day, although, I did hear from some others at the park that they are eating twice. It appears that the dogs are keeping their old schedules. Those of us without dogs before are fed once. I say "fed," although it is the humans doing the cooking and preparation, and the dogs deciding on the meals. They are adept at opening refrigerators and cupboards, pulling out packages, pointing, nudging, and letting us know what they expect us to prepare for them, anyway. We eat only dog food. The dry is tolerable. The wet is just gross. There are consequences for those of us who try to eat human food. One man was immediately banished to the backyard on a very short leash attached to a tall pole. He could only stand and was left there overnight.

Even worse than the food are the locked bathrooms. We are not allowed to use them. We are expected to go outside as the dogs do. They seem to get a hoot out of watching us. Frequently, several will gather to watch when one of us can't hold it anymore and goes behind a bush for relief. Sometimes they follow and stare. Showers are also a thing of the past and some of us are beginning to smell like ....well .... dogs. This morning, three of my neighbors jumped in the river, clothes and all. Their dogs sat on the bank and howled. Why this was happening to us is a mystery. There are many theories, most revolving around drugs in the drinking water, government conspiracies, and alien power mongers. Area 51 comes up a lot. I have no clue. But it is getting tiresome. I keep thinking this is a particularly vivid nightmare, and I will soon wake up in my own bed.

That doesn't happen. I wake up outside on the ground as do most of the others, leashes attached to the poles that are now everywhere. Fortunately it is warm weather. The dogs sleep in our beds. A few of us are permitted to sleep inside, mostly those who had dogs before. Those dogs seem to be mimicking their previous lives, allowing their humans to do what they were allowed to do. Those humans who made their dogs stay off the furniture are having a really rough time. One elderly man with bad knees is standing pretty much 24/7.

At the dog park, our leashes are secured on the poles. Those of us with long leashes can sit on the ground. Those with short leashes must stand. Why some are long and others short, we do not know. The dogs then go off and become their old selves, running, playing, doing dog things. The Great Danes use their big muscular necks to toss the Frisbees. A St. Bernard pulls back a tree limb while a German Shepherd pushes a tennis ball between two branches. The St Bernard lets it rip, and the Retrievers are off. A pair of Dobermans patrol the fence, several Terriers dig holes in pursuit of small mammals, and the Border Collie tries to herd everybody. Today, however, the dogs congregated in a large group barking, growling, and whining. There was also much howling until the Border Collie took charge. The others followed her lead, except for one Rottweiler who seemed to be challenging her authority. At one point he was "barked" down by the rest of the dogs and finally settled. The Retrievers did most of the "speaking," one at a time, mind you. The other dogs seemed to be listening intently, some chiming in with their own yips and barks. We don't know what's going on. We can only watch.

Today is day four, and we now know, we think, what all the discussion was about at the dog park yesterday. Most of us did not have electrified collars before today. Only a few "bad" humans had been subjected to them, mostly repeat resistors. Not anymore. This morning, every house was visited by either the Border Collie or one of the Retrievers, and the Big Dogs. Our choke collars were replaced with electrified versions. One little chomp on the leash and we are zapped. I blame the Retrievers. I think they pushed for it yesterday and convinced the others. What resistance there was, is now gone.

Today is the 7th day. The dogs dragged us all to the dog park early this morning and stayed with us this time, sitting quietly and waiting. So we, having no real choice in the matter, did the same. Suddenly a human appeared in front of us seemingly out of nowhere, laughing and applauding. We did not recognize him. The dogs did, though. Their tails wagged furiously. After a few moments, he began speaking, congratulating us, thanking us, even, for an exemplary performance. Finally he said, after millennia of failing to receive even an honorable mention, he was certain to take top honors in the Mischief on Remote Worlds category of the games. And it was all thanks to us. Then, POOF. He was gone. Human jaws dropped. Dog tails wagged even more furiously, and then suddenly, they were all jumping around, chasing tails and each other, yipping, yelping, and howling. It occurred to me that perhaps it was not the humans to whom he had been speaking. After a few minutes of celebration, the Border Collie barked three times, and the dogs ceased their antics and walked us back to our respective houses. We were all signing frantically at each other as we left. No one knew what it meant. Then, today around noon, the collars, leashes and poles disappeared. The dogs have gone back to being just dogs as near as we can tell. We can now speak and are gathering in groups to talk and compare. We all go quiet when we see a dog, watching, staring really, until he has moved on. Then we are all talking at once trying to figure it out.

It has now been 24 hours and all is still normal, but many are afraid it won't last. There was a town meeting last night, and already there is disagreement and arguing about what actually happened. A few claim it didn't happen. There are those who deny seeing the man in the park, and some who think he arrived and left normally – the rest of us just fooled by illusion. Some of us want to call the press, the police, or the FBI. Some even want to call NASA. I think it is pointless. Who would believe us?

News item in the New York Times later that summer
The Humane Society recorded an unusually large number of surrenders this month in a small town on the Maine coast. It appears that the residents of this town have given up every single one of their dogs. No reasons were given.

Ann Robinson

SPIRIT OF CHRISTMAS

Dog had been chasing Squirrel's family for what seemed like forever. Squirrel's first memory after leaving the nest was looking down on his parents racing across the ground pursued by a large brown barking dog. This was now a familiar daily sight. Dog never gave up and never won, except once. The Old One fell behind one day and was scooped up into the jaws of Dog. Miraculously, he survived, spat out onto the ground with a loud "dogful" BLECH. Apparently he was not the tasty morsel Dog had hoped for.

Even so, Dog returned day after day, chasing, barking and terrorizing the squirrel population. And to what end, Squirrel thought. It was such a waste of time and effort. No other animal would spend so much energy for no gain. Not if they wanted to survive. Not smart, in Squirrel's opinion. But then, in this case it didn't matter. Dog did not need to forage for food. He lived in the human house Squirrel could see from his tree, pampered, fed, and sheltered. No effort required. So Squirrel supposed Dog could afford to waste energy chasing him and his kin. And, if he was honest, it did keep his family on their toes and in shape. Others in the forest were not likely to spit out a slow squirrel. More likely it would be squirrel for lunch. He supposed he should be grateful to Dog.

Squirrel heard a door open in the human house and saw Dog run out on yet another squirrel hunt. He picked up an acorn in his jaws and started down the tree just as Dog arrived. Squirrel paused as Dog sniffed round and round the tree as he always did, then looked up, and spotted Squirrel. Dog stopped, still as rock, tail erect, eyes on Squirrel. Squirrel slowly descended until he was level with Dog. He paused, locked eyes with Dog, then dropped the acorn under Dogs nose and scampered back up the tree. Merry Christmas, Dog.

Ralph Neil Laughlin

Ralph's multi-faceted life experiences have given him a unique perspective and insight into the human psyche as reflected in his writings.

Born in Cedar Rapids, IA, he has lived in the Northeast, the Mid-Atlantic, the South, the Midwest and the West regions of the United States, plus over 15 years in Washington, DC, as well as spending extended periods of time in Europe.

A graduate of the University of Iowa, majoring in Journalism and Advertising, with a minor in Education, he went on to work for such global companies as General Electric, Texas Instruments, Fairchild Camera and Instrument, and eTERA Consulting. He's held major business negotiations with leaders of such notable Fortune 500 companies as Norte, AT&T, NCR, Chrysler, and Hewlett Packard.

Writing under the names of R. Neil Laughlin and R. Neil he has authored three books: *Beyond The Pool* – life lessons learned from swimming; *Random Thoughts Of A Wandering Mind* – reflections on today's world; and, *The Day The World Cried As One* – a compilation of individual remembrances of the day President Kennedy was assassinated. He has several others in the works.

Ralph Neil Laughlin

> *I'm new to Maine having only been here three years, and one of my biggest regrets is that I did not discover it earlier.*

LIVING IN THE STATE OF MAINE
Going from Here to There Sometimes Means Going Elsewhere

I was planning a trip from Brunswick, ME to Sarasota, FL. I thought it would be easy until I looked up the fare through major airlines. It seems all of them have decided that robbery on the high skies is most profitable, at least according to their rates.

My next step was to look at airlines using regional airports. That proved better. The fare was one third of the major airlines. The flight going south was out of Portsmouth, NH. That was perfect as there's regular bus service between Brunswick and Boston. I could just take the bus and get out at Portsmouth. The schedule said differently. No buses stopped at Portsmouth.

Okay, then I remembered Amtrak. I checked it out only to find it didn't stop in Portsmouth either. What's with Portsmouth that all modes of transportation steered clear of it?

I even looked at just renting a car to drive to Portsmouth, but the car rental agents seemed to be following the major airlines in their charges. I wish I owned a bandana company because I would be a millionaire by now with all the mask wearing crooks behind the counters in the travel industry.

Okay, to make a long story short, now that you're probably significantly bored with my story, I'll jump to the final agenda.
START TIME: Get up at 6 AM
Taxi: Home to Brunswick Station to catch the 7:20AM train
Train: Brunswick to Durham, NH
Taxi: Durham to Portsmouth airport and a 5 hour wait for a flight
Plane: Portsmouth to Punta Gorda, FL
Rental Car: Punta Gorda to Sarasota, FL
FINISH TIME: Approximately 7 PM
Then, in three days I get to reverse the whole schedule.

To conclude: "To go somewhere from Maine may take a lot of travel changes, but the big benefit is that when you're finished going, you get to come back to Maine. Yahoo!"

Ralph Neil Laughlin

I CAN'T BELIEVE EVERYTHING I THINK I KNOW

I'm a Man, therefore I know.
Just ask me and I'll tell you so.

On everything, I know where I stand.
My views are right and most grand.

I know what's right and wrong in our world,
I see it as one giant cultured pink pearl.

That's when she steps in and casts such doubt.
My fluid brain is suddenly in drought.

What I thoroughly thought was blue,
I'm told is not close to being true.

My brilliant mind flashes a blush,
having been rendered to mush.

So now before I say what I know,
I ask her which way I should flow.

I no longer need time to pause and think,
which gives me much more time to drink!

MATH OF EMOTIONS

Knowledge adds
Ignorance subtracts
Love multiplies
Hate divides

Ralph Neil Laughlin

I THINK…

Thoughts are cumulous clouds
of our emotions, of our feelings,
of what we've heard, read or said.
Sometimes light, joyous, exhilarating,
other times dark, dank, foreboding.
Sometimes soaring to the heavens,
other times burrowing under our skin.
Ever moving, ever evolving.
Rushing in and fading out.
Prime movers of change
within and without.
Accelerants, or retardants,
In our lives, our times, our world.
What do you think?"

What the worlds of cell phones and texting have done to the art of conversation.

CONVERSATION BETWEEN TWO 21ST CENTURY TEENS

    See?   *What?*
  Not what. *Huh?*
   There. *Where?*
   There! *Him?*
    No.   *Her?*
    Yea.   *Wow!*
    Hot.   *Nah.*
   Nah? *Sexy!*
   Yea! *Drip'n.*
 Gotta go. *'kay.*
   Later. *Later.*

Ralph Neil Laughlin

THE ARGUMENT IN FAVOR OF ACCUMULATIVE MATERIALISM

THE END

NOTE: Accumulation of wealth does not make a person a winner in life. The winners in life are those people who commit themselves to fully participating in the family of man; the people who say "Yes" to whatever circumstances they encounter on their journey through life. They reap the ultimate rewards from living, loving, laughing, crying and embracing life's offerings.

Ralph Neil Laughlin

WHERE HAS AMERICA GONE
Then
Kids playing outside on their own
Doors left unlocked all day
Open time to do whatever
People looking out for each other
Neighbors talking to neighbors
Public officers held in esteem
Politicians being civil servants
Public events joyful celebrations
Issues placed ahead of personalities
The Common Good, the common thread.

Now
Children being massacred in class
Homes made into fortresses
Everything to a schedule, a task
People indiscriminately attacked
Conversations held via machines
Public safety slain on the political alter
Public service now a career
Public events turned to hunting seasons
Personalities placed ahead of issues
Government's interest in special interests

Where has America gone...
and will we ever get it back?
The embers still linger
but must be fanned and flamed
to rekindle and rebuild our core
of Truth, Caring and the Common Good
for every citizen, rich or poor.

Ralph Neil Laughlin

These words came to me within a few days of the Sandy Hook Massacre. I'm still wondering where they came from.

THE TWENTY

They woke to a bright, promising new morn,
not knowing by evening their Nation would mourn.

They went to their school to be educated,
but instead became victims - eradicated.

They came full of vim, vigor and breath
but were carried out their school in the hands of Death.

They were someone's son or a daughter
turned into lambs led to slaughter.

They are now gone with barely a trace
helplessly we say "to a much better place".

Within a year of being laid down
they'll only be a memory in their hometown.

UNLESS, we choose to remember
that horrific day, the fourteenth of December.

Make it be a beginning to heal our wounded land
by letting go of the gun grip and extending a helping hand.

It is not about restricting a person's right to own a gun,
but of honoring each other's safety when all is done.

Ralph Neil Laughlin

> *A diagnosis of the affliction effecting Congress.*

PARTY POLITIC POX

Our country has contacted a serious disease
It's called the Party Politic Pox if you please.

Where politicians of the people don't give a rip;
instead, they're driven by their own Party's whip.

At the very first George Washington had said
Political parties will be the country's dread.

When did it happen? Neither you nor I know
but the life-threatening symptoms clearly show.

What was once Power to the People
has been distorted to Power to the Party.

The People have been forgotten and left behind
now simply fodder for the Party's wheel to grind.

We can only be saved by all giving a hoot
especially for our country's grass roots.

Speak out for what is right for our fellow man
Regardless of his religion or color of his hand

The professional politician needs to go
He's become the common people's foe

The professional politician needs to go
He's become the corporations' joe.

Select people to office who are people of reason
Not ones who just spout a Party's line of a season.

Ralph Neil Laughlin

We've been overrun by professional politicians
That's what leading to our country's attrition.

It's time to throw out the parties of waste
And bring back people with all due haste.

People who want to work for all together
and not just blow dark smoke and feathers

People who see the urgency of the case
ones who will act with all due haste.

People who believe in growing by compromise
people not hung up on dreams they idealize.

People who are anchored in true reality
not those dreaming wishful ideology.

Yes, our country is changing by religion and its tint
and if you don't believe it you haven't got a hint.

It's time to reclaim our true country the USA
away from those who chose to lead it astray.

By working towards our common needs and goals
not seeing each other as uncompromising foes.

Let's join hands to return things back to the right
By showing our blessed colors, red, blue and white.

ODE to a HUSBAND

After the children have come and gone,
One child stays and continues on.
Master of the house, ruler of the land,
yet always reaching out
for his wife's reassuring hand.

Ralph Neil Laughlin

SPRING

Spring has been asleep under winter's snow.
Today, its white blanket partially tossed as a throw
Revealing patches of chocolate-toned ground,
In places, covered by dark pine cones round.

Gray-blue boulders with tints of green
That jut out here and there over the scene.
Is the gentle slope curve of that hill
really Spring's exposed back to thrill?

Is she stretching to rise,
Or just turning to another side
To maintain her reside?

No buds have pushed forth,
nor blades of green grass
only bare tree branches
on the Willows and Ash.

Yet, greens of all shades
From the pine trees protrude,
giving color to the gray interlude.

Yes, Spring is awakening
She's starting to nest
It's just that she's not ready…
ready yet to get dressed.

Ralph Neil Laughlin

SNOW FALL

A snow fall is a most beautiful sight.
It's as if two giant hands
gathered up plump white clouds
and then began rubbing them together
to make fine flakes of white,
cascading down from the sky
to cover the earth with
a new coat of purity and delight.

ULTIMATE RESPONSIBILITY

YOU...
control success or failure,
through actions, deeds, commitments,
the ability to adjust to obstacles
fallen upon your chosen path
YOU...
determine your destiny of where you will be
be it good, bad or indifferently.
YOU...
make it happen or not.
It's up to YOU!

THE MOMENT

ENJOY the Moment because...
The Future is but speculation.
The Past is only a memory.
Only the Present is real.
ENJOY EVERY MOMENT!

Nancy Sohl

Nancy was born in St. Louis, but spent her early childhood in a small town in Massachusetts. When she was ten, her family moved back to the Midwest where she grew up in the suburbs of Chicago.

She graduated from Drake University in Des Moines, Iowa with a degree in elementary education, but came back to the Chicago area to teach school. She taught mostly 4th and 5th grade for 33 years before she and her husband, Ray, retired and moved to Maine.

They love the quiet, peaceful, beauty of their new home in Harpswell. They've been married 41 years now, and happily share their home with their golden retriever named Sally.

Nancy Sohl

THE BEST GIFT OF ALL

Once upon a time, deep in the snowy woods, there stood a very sad pine tree. Now this pine tree wasn't always sad. Most of the year he loved this quiet spot in the woods, but it was winter again, and the short cold days meant just one thing – Christmas was coming.

Christmas was a sad time for the little tree because it meant that once again he would be left standing in the cold instead of standing proudly in the window of a nice warm house decorated with beautiful ornaments and topped with a star. The birds had told him stories of the Christmas trees they had seen, but the little pine tree was just too far from town. No one would ever find him here. It would be another sad and lonely Christmas.

Now the little pine tree had many friends in the forest. He was loved by the birds that lived in his branches and the forest creatures that he sheltered from the wind and snow. They hated to see him so sad. So that Christmas Eve night, while the rest of the world slept, the forest animals worked hard to make this Christmas very special for their friend.

The birds gathered berries and pine cones to scatter on the branches of the little pine tree. The deer dipped vines in the pond so they would freeze and sparkle in the moonlight. They draped these icy garlands over his branches. A shooting star completed the effect.

That Christmas morning the little pine tree stood tall and proud, for his friends had transformed him. Thanks to their gifts he was truly a Christmas tree. He was beautiful because he was loved, and love is the best gift of all.

Nancy Sohl

REMEMBER WHEN

Remember when we read books on paper, and it was a joy to go to a book store and pick out a new one with rows and rows of shelves to choose from. I miss book stores.

Remember when our phone was just a phone. We didn't take pictures, shoot videos, watch movies, or access the computer with our phone. We just got and made phone calls with our phone.

Remember when we dressed up to fly on airplanes or go out to dinner. We dressed up to go to church, or to go to work, or to go to school. We dressed up a lot.

Remember when we kept in touch with friends through phone calls and letters. Sometimes we sent cards on special occasions, but we didn't Tweet, or Twitter, or Blog. (I do need someone to explain the difference between Twitter and Tweet. And while we're at it, could you tell me what a "hash tag" is.)

Remember when we went to the bank to make a deposit or get cash. To pay bills we wrote checks and put them in the mail.

Remember when our music was either on the radio or we bought an album – or later a CD. (I'm still not sure how to download music or what to download it to.)

Remember when we rode bikes without helmets, "carried on" liquids, didn't have so many ads on T.V. for sexual dysfunction issues and ate without thoughts of calories or fat or sugar.

Now don't get me wrong. I don't want to dress up for dinner. I don't want to give up my cable T.V. I enjoy e-mailing friends. I'm very happy to order a book for my I-Pad, and I think it's wonderfully amazing that if I need directions, my car can tell me where to go.

I'm all for seat belts and putting babies on their backs to sleep and screening at the airport (if I could just bring my shampoo and keep my shoes on). And I'm now paying attention to the SPF number in my sun tan lotion instead of using baby oil.

You've got to admit it was simpler then. We survived childhood untethered in the back seat of the car. We somehow made it to adulthood without every drawer, cabinet, bottle, and outlet being child-proofed. We didn't need computer games or movies in the car to amuse us. We had long-distance friends without Face Book, and we played outside with our friends after school instead of being inside playing video games.

I can't turn back the clock. I'm not sure I'd want to, but I do know in the world of my childhood we moved more, talked more, and I think, smiled more. We seemed to have more control over what came into our lives. Our world was smaller, but that was okay.

I can't even imagine what the future holds. It's changing so fast right now that I can't keep up. I would bet though that the kids of the future won't be able to imagine the world we grew up in either - and that's sad. It was a simpler time when we would sit with our parents or grandparents, and they would tell stories of their childhood that often began with, "I remember when …."

THE LITTLE THINGS IN LIFE

I've learned from my dog, a sweet golden retriever named Sally, to celebrate the little joys of life. Sally gets excited about belly rubs and the forgotten tennis ball rediscovered in the corner. She barks in eager anticipation of dinner even though it's the same food she gets every night. She wiggles and wags in delight when someone says, "Want to go for a ride in the car?" Sally's days are filled with little celebrations.

We moved from the Chicago suburbs to Harpswell two years ago. Since moving here, I've come to understand Sally's celebrations. The hummingbirds at my feeder and the bull frogs in the pond make me smile. I am awed by the beauty of the star-filled night skies, the picturesque bays and coves around every corner, and the snow that blankets the trees. Here the seasons are marked by the new lambs born at the farm, the lady slippers that bloom in the woods, the reopening of the lobster pounds, and the amazing colors of fall.

Life here is good. Sally and I both know now it's the little things in life that are worth celebrating.

Nancy Sohl

THE SEASONS OF OUR LIVES

I think there are so many good reasons
To compare our lives to the four seasons
If you're just lucky enough to live through all four
That should be enough – you'll not need or want more.

Spring is the birth of everything new
Early or late and often overdue
It can come in a rush, or a slow steady drip
Yes, it's spring and our birth that begins our life's trip

Spring can be a mess with rain (tears) and wet
You cry a lot, but your needs must be met!
There are warm sunny days filled with lots of giggles
Winds blow, the snow melts, and you're just full of wiggles

A time of firsts – first robin and tulip
First steps, first school, and first over-night trip
Spring is the promise of flowers, warmth, and bright sun
The spring of our lives is learning, growing, and fun

Then next comes summer – the best time of all
Done with school, on our own, having a ball
We got a job that pays well. We've picked out our spouse.
Maybe a family? And we found that dream house!

Summer is a time when all dreams come true
In summer there's nothing that you can't do
Sometimes there are storms that can ruin your day
But with the sun back out, you'll soon be on your way

Summer it seems might just last forever
What's not to like? It's the perfect weather
But there's pressure too with lots of bills to be paid
And we all know that summer sun is bound to fade

Nancy Sohl

Fall comes with bright colors and crisp, clean, air
The kids are now gone. You haven't a care.
But the nights can be cool and the days aren't so long
We're slowing down and there are some moans in life's song

On those crisp fall days, what could be better?
But you sense it's near - despite the weather
Yes, winter is coming with its snow and its cold
There's no way to stop it. You're about to get old!

At first it's just fine to cuddle inside
To escape the cold world, it's good to hide
It's so hard to get out, and there's not much to do
In the winter, the good days aren't many, but few

Your home is safe with your loved ones near by
You look at life with a contented sigh
Your work is all done. It's time to enjoy the past.
You're in no hurry now though. Try and make it last.

Enjoy each season with their good and bad
Their passing should make us happy, not sad
Our years are marked by seasons and our lives are too
Each season unique, a delight, making you – you

Nancy Sohl

CAMP SUNSHINE

I leave for camp tomorrow
It's the first time I'll be away.
They say I'll really like it there
But two weeks is a long time to stay

What if I really hate it?
What if I get sick while I'm there?
Will anyone come to get me?
Will there be anyone home to care?

What if I find a spider,
Or some big old bug, in my bed?
What if the food there is awful?
They may starve us with water and bread.

What if mosquitoes bite me
'til I swell like a big red ball?
Or we hike through poison ivy
And nobody at camp cares at all.

Camp Sunshine sounded so great
When we talked about this last year.
But now that I'm leaving tomorrow
I'm suddenly filled with doubts and fear.

Mom calls me her "what if" kid
I'm always expecting the worst.
I don't like that I think that way
It's not a blessing, it's just a curse.

I'll be brave and go to camp.
I'll be fine and camp will be fun.
Unless it rains each day I'm there…
Do they send us home if there's no sun?

SNOW DAY

    They say a blizzard is coming. We'll have a snow day for sure. It doesn't matter if you're six or sixty, there's something exciting about a snow day.

    There's plenty of warning. Weathermen have talked about its arrival for days. There's that rush to get to the grocery store along with everyone else getting milk and toilet paper. You fill your car with gas, and you wait.

    Like a kid you scan the skies. The day is here. What a great excuse to stay home safe and warm. It's a cookie baking day – a watch old movies day – maybe a mid-afternoon nap day. It's a snow day.

    Here it comes. It's soft and white, and the world is suddenly quiet and still. And then it's gone. The plows are out and the roads are clear. The sound of snow blowers fills the air. Where should we go? What should we do? Life is moving again.

    But wasn't it pretty? Wasn't it nice? A snow day made just for you to slow down and enjoy.

Winnie Silverman

Winnie was born and raised in Cleveland Ohio. She was appointed to the National Honor Society and graduated near the top of her high school class, but was not financially able to attend college. She then began her working life as a secretary. After marrying, she and her husband moved to the San Francisco Peninsula. They divorced after thirteen years of marriage and two children. Winnie then started a new life, along with her children.

She enrolled in Canada Junior College in San Mateo, California and achieved her AA degree with a 4.0 average (only the second person to do so), while working and taking care of her family. Then she began a career in Financial Services. To enhance her skills, she studied and became a Certified Financial Planner. After being successful in her work with clients, she was appointed Branch Manager at her firm. Five years later, she resigned and went into private practice, specializing in Financial Planning.

During her retirement, she moved to Maine to be near her daughter. When she joined the writers' group, Write On!, any writing outside of family memoirs was an entirely new experience. She is enjoying creating and sharing stories. She considers her greatest achievement to be her two children who both have attained Masters' Degrees and are personally and professionally successful.

Winnie Silverman

A CHARMING OLD COTTAGE

"Close to Bowdoin College," the ad said. "Three Bedrooms, One Bath." "This is a wonderful investment for you," urged my daughter. What she really meant was she needed a place to live with her very large dog. "You will make money while providing a place for me to live until I can get my own house." If you are a parent you can understand why I bought the place.

It was owned by a realtor, who had placed some well-chosen imitation antiques around the house. The larger bedroom was quaint with lace curtains, and the walls were covered with flower-patterned wallpaper. The small bedside table had a vase with a single flower. He sure knew how to dress up a house for eye appeal! Like the other rooms, it was small. We were too naïve to delve deeper into the plumbing, electrical and other inner workings of a house. It had passed inspection. Deb was in love! 'Nuff said.

Winnie Silverman

The Tour

The exterior was white clapboard except for an attached carriage barn which had weathered grey shingles on the side and back walls. There were two entrance doors to the house. The one in the center of the house looked like it had not been opened in years, and the painted wood was peeling. On the stoop, embedded in the concrete, was a metal boot scraper. The other door, which led to the kitchen, was the entry.

The attached carriage barn had double wood doors which were not square with the frame and were kept shut with a clasp and padlock.

Beginning the tour of the interior, the barn had a dirt floor. One door had a step up to the back yard. The other led to the kitchen. There were shelves along the interior wall and shovels and rakes propped against the door to the yard. There was a trap door leading down to a space containing a furnace.

The kitchen was very homey looking, had an electric stove, (probably vintage 1950's), nice wood cupboards, and a functional sink. By the window facing the street, there was room for a small table and chairs.

Next to the kitchen was the living room. There was a fireplace surrounded by a wood wall and mantel with two old sconces in the wall that at one time held candles. There was also a built-in bookcase and an unusual wood ceiling.

A staircase led upstairs. Next to it was another room which was called a sitting room. At the back of the room was another space that was oblong and narrow. It was no more than 6 or 7 feet wide.

Upstairs, as with many houses, one wall of each bedroom was slanted down to about 3 feet from the floor so that one could only stand up straight next to the interior wall. The bathroom, circa 1940, had the commode, sink and tub/shower, and attractive wood cabinetry.

Life in the Cottage

It was a cozy place, although Deb found there were some quirks involved with living in what was a very old house. Come along as she learns about living in her new home, room by room.

She knew a selling point was town water. No worry about a septic tank. Electric outlets and light fixtures were old fashioned but serviceable. She put a washer and dryer in the barn, but during the winter they were brought into the kitchen. In the kitchen, a table and chairs were placed by the front window. She bought a large side-by-side refrigerator and discovered that in order to get into it you had to move the kitchen table.

The living room was definitely charming and very livable. The wood burning fireplace had a modern glass screen and the heat spread around the entire downstairs. One of the two vents from the antique furnace was at the base of the staircase to the upstairs, but if the fire was lit there was no need for it.

The sitting room was most likely used as a bedroom before the upstairs was built. Deb put her computer in that room, and it was a pleasant place to work, with a front and side window. Leading out from the back wall was that long narrow room shelved for storing food but being used to dump anything she had no other place for. We wondered what the purpose was for this unusual space.

The stairs were very narrow and steep. Deb had to remove them to get her queen size mattress upstairs. We both bumped heads repeatedly forgetting not to stand up straight when getting out of bed. There was a floor board that always creaked on the way into the bathroom. The bathroom was very warm in winter because the upstairs heat vent was right next to the commode, and one could get burned by lingering there too long.

Deb rototilled almost the entire back yard to plant a lawn and vegetable garden. There is a good probability this soil had not been disturbed for a long, long time. She uncovered many pieces of metal, probably from carriages and also some pottery shards and a wedding ring. One could only wonder what the story was about that wedding ring.

Winnie Silverman

When I came to visit the following summer, there was a lush green lawn. Along one side there was a hammock and the pine trees in the back whispered in the wind. Paradise! Deb decided to do a barbeque for my visit. Unfortunately, the barbeque was too close to the siding and a good chunk of it melted. That exposed the old wood of the original structure. Prior to that we had assumed the clapboard was wood, but it was vinyl. Every spring, she also had to replace some wood shingles on the barn walls. She was a pretty good handyperson, which was certainly helpful with an old house.

Almost every day during my summer visits, a bearded man in cargo shorts and a safari hat walked down the street while reading a book. Neighbors said he was a professor at the college. Luckily, there was little traffic on this short street between a cemetery and the college.

There were some memorable times in that old house. Deb graduated from U Maine, and there was a big celebration. Also, my two sisters visited, and since we lived in three different states, it was quite an occasion.

History Revealed

There was an old woman who had lived next door all her life. She knew much of the house's history and enjoyed telling stories to Deb and then to me when I would visit.

To begin at the beginning, one room that was originally a bar was moved to the site. This became the living room in later years. The carriage barn was added, and then much later when plumbing and electricity were available, the kitchen was built between the two structures. The sitting room was another addition to the structure. "What about the room in back of the sitting room?" I asked. The old woman said that at one time a midwife occupied the sitting room and the narrow space in back of it was a birthing room.

The upstairs was built much later by raising the roof and then completing the supports and interior. This provided a bathroom and two bedrooms.

She then asked me if I had noticed the row of pine trees at the back of the property. I told her I admired them, and she said the son of Admiral Robert Peary had brought them from Peary Island, where he had retired.

I researched his story. Admiral Peary (1856 to 1920) was generally regarded as the first white man to set foot on the North Pole. The old lady told me a little girl named Marie was famous for being the first white child at the North Pole. I read that she was born in Greenland, and then lived at the North Pole for several years with her parents, the Admiral and his wife, Josephine. She played with the children of Inuit Eskimos who called her, The Snow Baby, and the newspapers picked up the story. I pulled a picture of a book cover from the internet showing her in heavy winter clothes.

THE SNOW BABY
The Arctic Childhood of Admiral Robert E. Peary's Daring Daughter
KATHERINE KIRKPATRICK

Then the old woman told me that when the girl had grown up, she lived for a while in our house. I can't verify any of her stories, but I doubt the storyteller could make all this up.

After about five years Deb was ready to move to her own home. It took me two years to sell the house as it seemed people didn't want a small, charming cottage that needed some work. A school teacher finally bought it, not for the charm, but for the price and location. By then the old woman had passed away, but I don't think the school teacher really cared about the house's history anyway.

A STREET GROWS UP

The sign at the entrance to the street says "Slow. Children at Play." It is a short dead end street. There is a path, an easement to the city, connecting to the next street. Neighbors' lawns on either side join that walkthrough to make an inviting place for kids to play. In front of one house across the street, Joe puts up a basketball hoop each year. This serves as an assembly point. Kids ride their bikes and skateboards or walk to meet there. Both boys and girls shoot hoops, just talk, or sometimes roughhouse. Sometimes a spontaneous game of baseball or soccer will begin on the green. Some kind of "radar" seemed to lure the kids from farther down the street. In today's world, it is most likely cell phones. Also, some older kids may lounge in the grass of the greenway just chatting, with their laptops open. Perhaps one generation has already moved out or gone on to college. As the years go by, fewer and fewer kids are out there, except they still do gather at the basketball hoop and shoot a few or just catch up with each other. Perhaps, in a few years, new kids will assemble and play on the street, but as the street has become older, perhaps not.

Winnie Silverman

A TREE GROWS IN CLEVELAND

    Every spring my mother bought seeds for a vegetable garden and about two dozen tomato seedlings. One year she also bought a maple tree seedling. Since my father wouldn't approve of her spending money for a tree, she hid it by planting it among the tomato plants.

    The tree grew inconspicuously year after year though my father didn't notice it. I watched it grow from my second story bedroom window. By the time I was a teenager, it was higher than my window. It was beautiful. I loved the wind rustling the leaves. It shaded my bedroom from the summer sun.

    Here in Maine, it is hard to believe a tree is such a special luxury that its purchase would be regarded as frivolous. Of course, there are already plenty of trees in the Pine Tree state; however, some valid reasons to buy a tree might be for new landscaping or replacement for a sick or dead tree. Nurseries do manage to sell them. The shade of tall trees here in my back yard in summer is as welcome here in Maine as it was in Cleveland.

Karen Schneider

Karen Schneider is a freelance writer and editor who loves lupines, sea roses, and concocting delicious food for family and friends in her kitchen. When she's not writing or daydreaming, she's off adventuring with her grandchildren.

Originally from Upstate New York, she has lived in Mid-coast Maine for over 30 years and is the mother of four children. Karen is a regular contributor to *The Times-Record and The Lewiston-Sun Journal.* She also works with other authors as an editor.

Karen Schneider

MY DAUGHTER, KATE

My daughter, Kate, picks berries.
From July through September she
Offers brimming baskets to me
With stained fingers and her
Sticky mouth grins at me on
Ocean blue days as she takes
The best Maine summer has to offer.
Wild strawberry sun glints her hair and
Thorns of raspberries tear at her legs.
Mosquitoes like her best at
Dusk in the blackberries…
Yet she picks on
While the forever
Autumn person that I am
Stands at the stove turning jars
Into the elegance of stained glass
My fingers taking on purple and
Crimson hues…
On a dull winter morning I'll
Reach for a cool ruby jar
Open it
And taste her summer smile.

Karen Schneider

THE SUNDAY TRADITION

This past Sunday, I stopped in at Dot's in Bath for a mocha fudge ice cream cone. After plunking down three bucks and leaving fifty cents in the tip jar, I strolled back to my vehicle to savor my purchase thinking about how this summer-time treat has been part of my life ever since I can remember.

This favorite family tradition was started long ago by my parents who were almost as religious about taking us to the Fair Haven Dairy Bar on Sunday afternoons as they were about getting us to Mass earlier in the day.

Since I was the oldest, I was often the one to stand at the Dairy Bar's window with my father's hard-earned dollar bill clutched in my hand, ready to issue the family's order, a monumental task. My parents often made it easier by ordering the same thing which was usually a large size maple walnut for twenty-five cents, though sometimes Dad had a hankering for butter brickle, or Mom craved orange pineapple or black raspberry. (I won't soon forget the auspicious day my littlest sister discovered mint chocolate chip. I do believe it was the first time I beheld a human being in absolute ecstasy.)

I had my favorites too, with chocolate and fudge ripple at the forefront, although occasionally I was in the mood for lemon or orange sherbet and was thrilled beyond belief when rainbow sherbet was invented. I wasn't as excited as the rest of the family when the Dairy Bar procured a soft ice cream machine, however. To this day, I feel strongly that ice cream should be hard and very cold, not soft and too quick to melt into a puddle.

What I remember most about those Sunday sojourns is how grown-up and responsible I felt as I stood in line amongst the townies and tourists, holding that dollar. After carefully delivering the cones two at a time and returning the dime in change, I sat in the car with the rest of the family while Dad regaled us with his stories. We all had a lick of each other's frozen treats and "kissed" our ten-cent, medium-sized cones which meant bumping one another's ice cream together gently just enough to have a dollop of the different flavor against our own. When we were finished, Mom wiped us up with the wet washcloth she'd brought along. Then we headed for home feeling satisfied beyond measure.

Years later, when I started a family of my own, I made it a point to carry on this fine Sunday tradition. Upon our arrival in Maine twenty-six years ago, one of my first missions was to find the nearest ice cream stand. Our family has its favorites, but the one we frequented most when my daughters were small was the Richmond Dairy Bar. After we moved from Bowdoinham to Topsham, we became regulars at Dairy Queen on Main Street, and one special summer my daughter, Katie, had the distinction of being employed at Cote's in downtown Brunswick. You better believe we made many visits to that fine establishment and still do to this day.

Now that my girls have all grown up and especially since my waist has grown a tad wider, I don't eat ice cream every Sunday anymore, but when I do I can't help but recall those long-ago, carefree days of my youth, how the pavement of the Fair Haven Dairy Bar parking lot warmed my bare feet, and how, for less than a dollar, our family of six feasted on the creamy, cool elixir of summer.

ONCE

I left myself on a dirt road in Maine
Where the grapevine and raspberries
Tangle together
And the thistle pokes its fuzzy head
Through infertile soil.

My heart is in the house where
The kitchen door yawns open
And the roof sags down.
Here I once pounded nails
And dreamed dreams.

Karen Schneider

A SUMMER PLACE

When I was twelve years old, my father built a screened porch on the back of our house in the shade of a black walnut tree. It was a simple structure with a plain wood floor, a picnic table, and a few old wicker chairs. The family often gathered there on hot summer evenings to feast on steak, chicken, or hamburgers that Dad cooked to perfection in the outdoor barbeque pit. You could also find us there on Sunday mornings eating pancakes, bacon, and eggs before church. It was my job to set the table and carry out the toaster from the kitchen. I loved making the toast and buttering it right at the table, then eating it while it was still crisp and hot and smothered in homemade jam.

Although it was nice to be gathered together for a family meal, my favorite times on the porch were spent alone during the early morning hours, even before my mother made the coffee and mixed the pitcher of Tang, even before my dad drove off to work in his pick-up. The eldest of four children, I needed as much quiet as I could find, so I made the screened porch my own in the brief pocket of time when the remnants of night gave way to the pinky-silver glow of another new day. Sitting in my summer nightie with my bare feet tucked under me, I listened to the birds and watched the dew dry on the grass. I wrote poetry in a black and white speckled notebook as I daydreamed, waiting not only for that day to begin, but for the rest of my life and all its wonderful possibilities to unfold.

The screened porch was reincarnated many times after I left home. Over the years, my dad, who was a carpenter, improved it, expanded it, and renovated it. Finally, professional contractors created a spacious showplace that could be used year-round. The sunroom, with its expanse of windows, flickering gas stove, and cushiony chairs, became the heart of the house, not only in summer but in winter, spring, and fall.

For years and years, I've carried the ache of wanting a screened porch. Living in nearly fifteen different homes in five states, as well as in another country, I never once had any type of "summer place". I fantasized about a space with windows thrown open to the ocean breezes; a room to decorate with wicker furniture where I could drink lemonade, play Parcheesi, or read trashy novels; a place to rock on a creaky glider and listen to the birds.

I scraped together all my money and called a builder. I hired him because he reminded me of my dad. Now for the first time in my adult life, I have a summer place. Not as large and plush as the final version of my parents' sun room, yet fancier than that screened porch from my childhood. My sun porch looks over the marsh with its resident eagle, blue herons, and red-winged blackbirds. There's a wicker chair with a fluffy cushion, a couch for afternoon naps, a stack of books, a table for family meals, and a toaster I can leave right there.

Spending my evenings serenaded by peepers and crickets, I watch for fireflies and contemplate the glittering galaxy. I preside over family cook-outs that include little children brimming over with laughter as they run out into the yard to play in the sprinkler, slamming the screen door behind them.

Most of all, I cherish the early morning hours. I get out of bed and start the coffee before I unlock the door. Then I go to my summer place. With my spiral notebook and pen in hand, I tiptoe across the wood floor in my bare feet to witness the sun rising in a pinky-silver glow as the dew dries on the grass. I make toast, pour coffee, then settle in to witness yet another day unfolding into countless glorious possibilities.

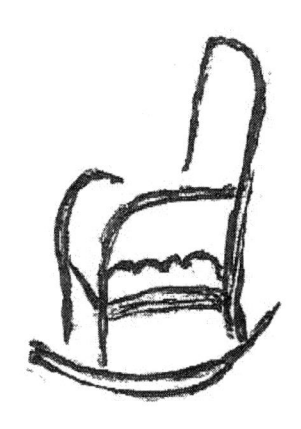

Vince McDermott

Vince was born in Trenton, NJ, too many years ago, he says, and now lives in Brunswick with his wife, Joanne. They moved to Maine in 1998. He was a meteorologist for thirty years, serving in the USAF and working for the National Weather Service as well as in private industry.

Vince wrote many nonfiction articles on stamp collecting before joining Write On! in 2005. He now writes poetry, historical fiction, tales about strange happenings, and stories about life in Maine.

He has contributed fiction pieces to magazines, recited at poetry readings, and continues to write articles.

Vince McDermott

I WROTE A POEM

I wrote a poem
Didn't like it
But it had something
I passed it on

My writing group
Didn't like it
But there was this thing
I passed it on

The local paper
Didn't like it
But the thing was still there
I passed it on

The poetic journal
Didn't like it
Was something really there?
I passed it on

My wife read it
She liked it
There was something there
I am a poet laureate

Vince McDermott

UNCLE BENNY'S VISIT

My wife and I had finished Sunday dinner early in November and were settling in for a quiet evening at home around 7 when the doorbell rang. I got up grumbling from my comfortable chair and went to the door. When I opened it I got a shock. It was Benny, my wife's uncle. I got a brief view of a taxi pulling away.

Benny was not my wife's real uncle. We weren't really sure exactly what his relationship to my wife was. Benny had been born in a village in eastern Poland which had been obliterated by the German and Russian armies during World War II. All of his immediate family had been killed. Somehow Benny escaped and made his way to a town where a cousin lived. Benny was ten at the time. He lived with the cousin for a while, and then both had to get away from the advancing Russians in 1944.

At first they lived with relatives in southern Poland where the cousin died. Benny eventually joined the flood of refugees which flowed into Western Europe. He eventually made it to the United States. Benny had to work hard to survive, so he didn't get much education. He was good with his hands and was able to get many jobs repairing almost anything. He never married and lived mostly in rented rooms. He did not speak English well and had hearing problems. He smiled a lot to hide his deficiencies.

Benny came into my wife's life, late in his. He had been having a number of medical problems resulting from his rough life during the war. Over time, all relatives who helped him passed away, except for my wife who was apparently a cousin about six times removed. Reluctantly, she took over his care, and was able to get him into a group home where he lived for a number of years. We had not heard from him for some months.

Now here he was - at our front door. I invited him in and asked how he was. He didn't say anything, just smiled. I led him to a chair. My wife came in and stopped. She couldn't believe Benny was here. She had been trying to get him to visit for years.

Benny sat down but was visibly agitated despite his smile. My wife asked him if he wanted something to drink. No response, just another smile. Suddenly, he got up and turned to leave. We didn't know what to do. Had we offended him? He went to the door, turned and smiled and went out. I looked and saw a cab in the driveway. It was obviously waiting for Benny. He got into the cab, and it drove away.

My wife and I were dumfounded. She decided to call the home to see if they knew anything. She talked for a few minutes, then hung up. When she turned around, she was white. I asked what the matter was. She was visibly shaken and had to sit down. When she told me, my knees got weak and I sat down too. Benny usually took a short walk in the evening when it was still light. But today, on the first Sunday in November, daylight saving ended. It got dark earlier. Benny had been walking on his usual round but apparently got confused in the darkness. As he tried to cross a street, he was hit and killed - by a taxicab.

COLD MOONLIGHT

Cold front passage
Crisp clean air
Ice crystals sparkling
Stars shining brightly

Full moon rising
Over quiet pond
Shimmering silver rays
Reflecting off water

Lone creature walking
Over frozen ground
Crinkling steps
Stream coming from nostrils

Brushing against
Ice laden firs
Broken shards falling
Breaking on hard ground

Moving over fallen snow
Large tracks left
In my yard
Mystery to be solved

Vince McDermott

THE STORM

    The first snowflake fell around 10 AM. Most of the forecasters and computer models were in agreement about the storm. It was going to be small, and it would move fast. At first everything went according to plan. Light snow fell from late morning into the afternoon. Things started to go awry just before rush hour. The snow fell faster. The plows were able to keep up for a while, then rush hour traffic began to slow them down. They fell behind. There were a number of fender benders. Traffic slowed to a crawl and, in some places, it stopped completely.

    The snow continued to fall. The storm center defied the forecasts as it slowed and intensified. I had arrived home late in the afternoon and was able to follow the storm. Things got progressively worse. TV stations aired a long list of cancellations. By midnight, at least a foot had fallen, and there was no end in sight. I dozed in front of the fire, leaving the TV on. Every time I awoke, the snow totals were higher - two feet, then three. I finally decided to go to bed.

    In the morning I got up and wondered how much snow had fallen. I looked out the window and could not believe what I saw - nothing! No snow. What was going on? Then I realized what had happened. It was just a dream. Was I relieved.

    I had overslept and had to rush to get ready for work. I watched TV as I quickly ate breakfast. All the forecasters were talking about a snowstorm. The forecasts were in agreement. It would be a quick mover. I began to get uneasy. I looked out the window. Nothing yet. I got dressed and opened the door. The first snowflakes were falling. I glanced at the clock. It was 10 AM.

Vince McDermott

STRAWBERRY SEASON

Strawberry season is here! UMMMMM. Strawberries. I'm going to put them on everything - cereal, ice cream, salads, and waffles. I can use them in cakes, pies, and cookies. I can eat them by the handful. Is that stand down the road open yet? I can get them there. I'll buy several boxes to start with.

What a terrific year! The berries are plump, juicy, and very tasteful. They may not last long. I'll have to get more before they run out. There is plenty of room in the fridge. I should finish off some of the older ones before they go bad. Lots left. Maybe the people next door would like some. I shouldn't let them go to waste. I guess I bought too many.

I never want to see another strawberry. Hey! Blueberry Season is almost here. UMMMMMM. Blueberries.

GROUNDHOG

Oh fickle furry fiend
Indecisive, unreliable, overrated
Living a life of luxury
Pampered, coddled, cared for

You raise our hopes
Or dash them
Sunshine or shadow
More winter or less

One day of work
Such a deal
What do you do
The rest of the year?

A solution to
The problem
Is plain to see
Groundhog fricassee

Vince McDermott

BE CAREFUL WHAT YOU WISH FOR

Thornton Clarkson had a little too much to drink at the office Christmas party. He had been on the verge of telling one of the senior partners what he thought of him, but after thinking it over, he decided not to and walked unsteadily to the elevator.

He got off the elevator, signed out, nodded to the security guard, and looked out the big front window. Great! It was snowing. He knew he would never get a cab, so he started to walk home. Ordinarily, it would be a short jaunt, but in his condition it would be difficult, especially in the storm. He usually followed the same path every evening, but he decided to take a short cut to get some protection from the snow and wind.

He figured he couldn't get lost, even in storm conditions. He turned into a side street which looked familiar. The storm was getting worse - much worse. It was bitterly cold, and Thornton was wearing only a light overcoat and no boots. He trudged on but knew he had to find shelter. He realized he didn't know where he was. The snow was getting deeper and the visibility was worsening.

He wasn't sure what to do. At first, he thought all the stores on the street were closed. Then he saw a dim light in a shop window. There was a faded sign on the door. He was barely able to read it in the gloom - "The Wish Shop." It really didn't matter. He had to get into some place warm – and soon.

He opened the door. A bell in the back store tinkled faintly. He moved to a counter which took up most of the space in the tiny room. He noticed that there were no goods on display. What kind of store is this? He had warmed up a lot and was getting ready to leave when a very old man came out of the back through tattered curtains.

"Good evening sir. Nasty night out."
"Sure is. At least it's warm in here. What kind of store is this?"
The old man smiled. "Perhaps it is what you want it to be."
Thornton was puzzled. "What do you mean?"
"Didn't you see the sign on the door? I deal in wishes."
Thornton looked at the old man. The guy was serious. "You grant wishes?"
"In a way."

I'll play his silly game thought Thornton. Besides, it was warm in the shop. "What do you charge?"

"If the customer is satisfied, the customer will reward me."

This is getting ridiculous, thought Thornton. I'll call his bluff. What Thornton wanted was warmth and lots of it. No beaches though - too boring. He was a history buff. He was particularly interested in the glories of ancient Rome.

"OK. Send me back to ancient Rome at the time of the circuses in the Coliseum." At least I'll be warm.

The old man hesitated, thought a few minutes, then reached under the counter. He picked up something and handed it to Thornton. It was a small vial containing a yellow substance.

"Pour some of it unto your hand."

"What is it?"

"Sand from the Coliseum."

Sure, thought Thornton. I'll bet. But it looked harmless. He poured some unto his hand. This must be a joke. Then he saw a mist forming around him. The store was fading into the mist. He was completely enveloped. He felt weak and light headed. He sank to the floor and passed out.

After a while Thornton revived and stood up. The mist began to fade. He didn't know where he was. Then he heard the roar of a huge crowd. They were cheering! He felt something under his feet. It was sand - the same kind of sand that was in the vial. Could it be? Could he be in the Coliseum in ancient Rome?

The mist cleared completely. Yes, he was there. He saw the crowd. The noise was deafening. He sensed movement behind him. He turned - and screamed. A lion was there - ready to pounce.

Thornton had gotten his wish.

Vince McDermott

THE ADVENTURES OF SIR SNIDELY

Prologue:
    Sir Snidely was one of the worst villains in English history. His own biographer, Courthright Farnesworth, who helped him write his work, described him as a dastard, cad, thief, rogue, and blackguard. Quite soon after that, Snidely seduced Courthright's sister and stole thousands from him.
    Here are a few excerpts from the "Adventures of Sir Snidely."

Sir Snidely's Revenge Thwarted

    Sir Snidely galloped into the courtyard on his foam flecked black steed. The horse's hooves clattered loudly and echoed off the surrounding walls. He reined in hard, cruelly cutting into the stallion's mouth. *I'll remember that*, thought the horse. Snidely leaped off the mount and crashed heavily onto a nearby flower bed. His well polished boots crushed a row of fragrant blossoms. *I'll crush that upstart Utter just like I crushed those flowers*, thought Snidely. His black eyes narrowed while his mouth twisted into a hideous grin. His moustache twitched menacingly.
    Snidely strode rapidly toward the main house. He thrust open the French doors and entered the parlor. He came to an abrupt halt. There before him was Lady Daphne, the most beautiful woman in the whole shire. Another reason to hate Derek Utter. For some strange reason which Snidely couldn't fathom, Daphne favored Utter over him, Sir Snidely, one of the most dashing, handsomest, charming…you get the picture.
    "Where's Utter?" growled Snidely.
He saw fear in her beautiful violet eyes. She backed away, but was blocked by the piano. No music lover, Snidely was suddenly grateful that Daphne's family was musical.
    "He…he isn't here," whispered Daphne.
Well, well, well, thought Snidely. *Utter is doing me a favor by being absent.* He took off his hat and flung it away. He slowly approached Daphne. Her eyes widened. He unbuckled his sword belt and let it drop. It clanged when it hit the floor. Daphne flinched and raised her hand as if to ward him off.

"D…Derek will be back soon," she stuttered.

Not soon enough, thought Snidely. He got closer to the vision of loveliness. Daphne took a deep breath and almost swooned. The jaded Snidely gasped as her twin mounds of unblemished ivory strained against her dress. *Enough!* He lunged forward, reached out with both hands, grasped the edges of her brocaded gown, and…

At that moment, in the nick of time, Derek Utter entered the room. He grasped the situation immediately. That was unusual, since Derek wasn't that swift. He drew his sword and advanced on Snidely.

"Unhand her Snidely, you foul villain."

Oh, gad, thought Snidely. *Who's writing this drivel?*

"Well, Utter, you have provided me with a rare opportunity since you have drawn your sword. Now, I can run you through in self-defense." He reached for his sword and…uh, oh…he'd forgotten that he had dropped his sword. He backed away and took a different tack. He sneered at Utter. Sneering was one of his best weapons. He practiced it every morning as he shaved. A sneer was better than a smile. He'd sneered down many a tradesman and creditor.

Derek didn't fall for it. He lunged forward and slashed Snidely's very expensive embroidered coat. Snidely blanched. That wouldn't do. He'd spent too many hours groveling for the money to pay for the coat. He was very good at groveling, since he was always low on funds and had to continually beg, borrow, or steal from anyone available. He'd drunk countless cups of tepid weak tea and eaten crustless, tasteless sandwiches in the dank, dismal house of his aunt, the dotty dowager Duchess of Dorset, waiting for her to begrudgingly bestow on him a few gold coins.

Snidely quickly evaluated the situation and decided to fall back. Another slash would ruin the coat completely. He was too proud to do more groveling. He had some pride left. Not much, but some.

Derek pressed in, waving his sword.

"Wait, Derek." It was Daphne.

What's this, wondered Snidely*? Is she having pity on me or is she just afraid of getting blood on the carpet? What was she up to?*

Karen Johnson

Karen Johnson is a retired educator who taught writing to children and adults in Maine schools and universities for over thirty years. Retired from teaching, she writes for the children of the children she taught. Her latest endeavor is the novel *Singing Bird: Molly Ockett, a Maine Legend*. For details go to www.singingbirdnovel.com.

Karen Johnson

THE BEAR WHO CAME TO MY HOUSE

Mom was yelling for me to get up, but I just burrowed deeper into the covers. "I'll be down in a minute," I replied, not wanting to put my warm feet on the cold floor.

She hollered again, "Look out the window. There's a surprise waiting for you outside."

I opened one eye, sprawled over the edge of the bed and pulled the shade up a bit. Two inches of snow rested along the outside windowsill. I whooped, "Snow!! Finally." I raised the shade and saw at least two feet had fallen overnight.

Fully awake, I rummaged in the dresser for wool socks, sweater, and ski pants, not caring if they matched. I was in a hurry to get outdoors. After a green Thanksgiving, a brown Christmas, and an icy New Year, I was finally looking out at a Christmas card wonderland.

A frosting of white glistened on the laden fir branches, the garage roof, the shed roof, and the driveway. Rows of snow perched on the fence rails, and the posts wore white hats. Miniature towers formed on the tops of clothespins left on the line, and the pendant pin cherries huddled in bunches under their little snow blankets. It was perfect snowball snow. The lawn was white and flat and smooth except for a row of holes.

Holes? Holes! Big holes. Too big for dog tracks and too round for boot prints. I saw that they went from the edge of the woods to the garbage can. I galumphed down the stairs, slipped on boots, jacket, hat and mittens, and slammed out the door leaving the tantalizing smell of maple syrup behind.

From a distance the holes looked like a row of salad plates set out on a white tablecloth. As I got closer, I could see that they were deep footprints and very close together. Each was bigger than my hand. There was a sharp claw mark at the end of each toe. It had to be a big bear going very, very slowly after a long winter's nap. I looked to see where the bear went after failing to open the can, but that was where the tracks stopped.

Karen Johnson

Then I heard a scraping sound coming from the can which was only three or four feet away. I stopped breathing and backed around the corner of the garage. I peeked out cautiously and watched the lid on the pail jiggle, then pop up. What emerged looked a bit like a sombrero hanging over a shiny black nose, two beady eyes, one furry face, and a very wet, yawning tongue. But it wasn't a big bear at all, it was just a cub. I stared at the cub, and he stared at me for a moment, then tipped the pail over and tumbled out grabbing a plastic margarine tub in his mouth. I felt like Sal in the book *Blueberries for Sal** which reminded me that where there is a cub, there is probably a mama bear.

A warm breath suddenly puffed in my ear, and I jumped at least six feet straight up in the air. I came down running and made for the door. Flying up the front steps, I passed Mom headed down in the direction of the garage swinging a broom. Sam, our cowardly dog, hid under the porch and barked. I crashed through the door and threw open the casement window to cheer Mom on.

What a sight. Still carrying the margarine tub, the cub had one foot stuck in a coffee can and was hobbling into the woods trying to shake it off. Mama bear was cuffing the cub along, braying louder than Sam. Mom was swatting at the bears with the flat of the broom and screaming like a banshee.

From my safe vantage point inside, I thought this was the funniest thing I ever did see, and I howled until tears ran down my cheeks and my sides ached. Mom sure was right about that surprise.

*(Robert McCloskey, Viking Press, 1948)

Margie Kivel

Margie Kivel is a poet, essayist, and artist living in Rockport, Maine. She has had work published in The Lampeter Review: Journal of the Lampeter Creative Writing Centre, Trinity St. David, Wales; the Stanza, a tri-annual publication of the Maine Poets Society; and in two monthly on-line publications – Nourish Magazine and The Flint Spiritual Church Newsletter. Margie is a member and the Membership Chair of the Maine Poets Society, and is also a member of two writing groups – Write On! in Brunswick, and High Tide Poets in Rockland.

She says of her work: *I have been doing word pictures, written, or drawn for as long as I can remember. One of those explosions blasting through the cannon of life experiences gave me a jump start 5 years ago, and here I am. Nature makes me ponder, life makes me wonder, and between the two, the pen flows. It's a heady experience that sometimes makes me grateful for the cannon.*

Margie Kivel

A DAY'S CATCH

This new and exciting turn
of events can be as small as
marbled-green moths clinging,
clinging to my window screen,

or as large as the returning
wave of color and song –
warblers in the spring,
doorways to new worlds.

Today the viburnum
has white ballerinas
dancing the length of
outstretched branches.

This morning there was
a fox in the apple tree.
I did not see what came before,
only the eventual leap down.

Birds and wind have sown
sways of color in the fields,
the gift from last year's bounty
distributed with a heavy hand.

Would that I had eagle eye
to take in a broader
swathe of abundance,
to savor even more delights,

or be the tiny ant and see
the world from its perspective,
feel the soft petals under foot
and taste the sweet honey dew.

Margie Kivel

AGAINST THE GRAY

Men lift long, yellow poles,
banging them together;
plastic jousting sticks
tossed into pickup bed.
Flashing lights signal
clean up in progress,
note winter's final defeat.

In my space across the tracks,
rolling sounds are brewing
a perky cup of tea,
over which language
of arrival takes place.

Red house finch against the gray
reminds me of the sweetness
of its song in spring,
goldfinches waxing yellow
in the skinny light.

One by one,
winter locks snap–
sound of life's return.

Margie Kivel

WINTER CANDY

A flash of speckled white
drifted overhead, flew across the dump.
Flap of long wings and flat profile…

and a flash of recognition – owl!
In particular, snowy owl, come down
from the arctic in search of food.

News called it an eruption. I saw
winged visitations, owls landing
on roof and tree tops, airport runways –

falling gumdrops for hungry eyes
until green's main meal in spring.

CLOUD DREAMING

Emerging from a mass
of bunched clouds, they come,
a dancing school – sleek
fish leaping the sky.

Could be porpoise
or small minke whales,
depending on my
cloud imaginings.

Below them a thin line
of alizarin crimson,
then the dark grays
of their airy water.

Tomorrow holds another
day for cloud cinema,
never a rerun, always fresh,
unless the blue wins.

Margie Kivel

MORNING-AFTER GHOSTS

Crows pause frozen in sky,
wings parallel to bodies, breast
scooping updrafts for lift.

Wind pockets wind up the trees,
grabbing leaves by limb full;
up Mount Battie, fog roils overhead.

Two young boys fly down street
on skate boards, reckless and
shirtless, but wearing helmets.

Bent old man teeters on curb,
praying wind comes at his back,
gives a push across the street.

Dad shoulder-hugs his phone, walking
into the wind, baby's arms in stroller
are open wide with joy.

Herds of gray clouds hang low,
roam the sky, corralled by
wrap-around buildings.

Hunker-down Halloween drapes
over the streets, morning-after
ghosts loiter in shrubs.

Margie Kivel

STEP BY STEP

    I look behind me and you are there,
sitting on the back porch steps
of a sunny black and white day –
they call you "Daddy's girl."

I look behind me and you are
racing the wind, known to all as
"the fastest girl on the playground –
she lived on air to be *light."*

I look behind me and find that
you are hidden among the trees.
Something has been lost
within that step to woman.

I look behind me, there you are
hillside searching for the dream time;
awake and in your sleep, you ask
"where did it go beyond the edge?"

I look behind me, and you're wearing
the map of love on a rocky coast,
with its jagged curves and sags,
diving with the ducks for fish.

I look within, and gather
loosely those separations of
you and me, becoming one
in time for one more reel.

Margie Kivel

OCTOBER FLUSH

The scene appears to be serene,
still, save for occasional leaf falls,
breeze that ruffles shrub and fern
in passing through.

Ground suddenly begins to move
in fits and jerks--tiny sumo wrestlers,
white throated sparrows toss
leaves larger than they,
doing a tap dance chug
to find what lies below.

The landscape is alive with movement,
all quick hops, bursts
of elfin energy following
late summer's torpor;
leaping from the page of fall
for the last hurrah.

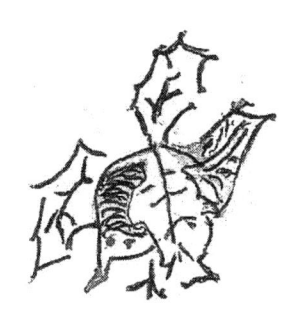

Margie Kivel

TELL ME HOW YOU CAME TO BE

I want to know what was seen,
words heard and tears wept,
how life fed back redeemed
that which was later kept.

Tell me of your passage
across the sea's expanse,
moments of starless nights
and fish that sing and dance.

No fisherman's tales
of what was caught,
but memories revealed
and tangents sought.

Speak into and through my eyes
of rumbling underneath,
during calm upon the surface
when mind drifts off to sleep.

Each realm of your existence
speaks of and to my own,
as we touch upon the waters
before our journey home.

Margie Kivel

WEEKEND RITUAL

Saturday at the Farmer's Market,
buyers looking for more
than food for money.
They bring their dogs, reusable
bags and a hunger
that needs filling –
like a museum art attack,
exposure to raw creativity
that feeds the soul,
But here, under tents
among vivid colors
and shapes of produce,
artisan breads, farm cheese,
lulled by the drone of conversation,
fiddles and thin flat voices
of old time singing,
balance is restored in gratitude
for those who work the land with love.

Beth Compton

Beth was born in Farmington, Maine, in 1962. After graduating from high school she started working at the IGA in 1982. In 1999 she moved to Brunswick and started working at Hannaford. She worked in the deli department for 9 years before switching to the store front where she has been for about 5 years.

Beth joined the Write On! group in 2010. She enjoys writing about her personal experiences.

Beth Compton

BOBBY'S SPECIAL CHRISTMAS

There was a little boy named Bobby. He had always wanted a puppy. Then one Christmas morning, he woke up and went downstairs to the Christmas tree and, to his great surprise, found a puppy in a box. He yelled, "Mommy, Daddy, I found a puppy in a box!" His mom and dad came running down the stairs. Bobby asked," Is this puppy mine?" His mom and dad answered, "Yes, he's all yours." Bobby was so happy! He gave his mom and dad a great big hug and said, "Thank you very much. I have always wanted a puppy!" He named his puppy Rusty. He played with Rusty all day. His mom said, "Bobby, you have more presents to open," but Bobby was too occupied with his new puppy to want to open anything else. Besides, it was time for supper.

After Bobby ate and had his bath, he was ready to go to bed. As he went upstairs, he called his new friend. Rusty followed him, and they both went to sleep cuddled together and had sweet dreams.

.

A DARK STORMY NIGHT

It was s a dark stormy night. It was a dreary night. The wind was howling. The branches on the trees were going snap, snap, crackle, pop. The leaves were falling everywhere. The lights were out all over. There were things going bang, crash. Things were flying everywhere. There was a loud scream, yelling, yelling, "Help, help, help."

Then you heard nothing…only the howling of the wind.

THE MOONLIT NIGHT

It was a bright moonlit night
The moon shining so bright
The stars glistening in the sky
What a beautiful sight.
It was such a lovely night.

Beth Compton

PENNY THE SNEAKY CAT

Penny loved to get into things and loved to get under foot. She liked to do things when she thought she wasn't being watched.

"Penny, I see you. If you think that I'm not looking, you're wrong. You love to be sneaky, don't you? And you love getting into trouble. You're such a crazy and funny cat that it's hard telling what you're going to do. You enjoy getting into things that you shouldn't, you know. No matter how many times you do the things you do, I love you, anyway."

THANKSGIVING

Time for turkey, pumpkin pies,
Chocolate cream pies, and all the fixings,
So good, all the tummies full,
Yum, yum, yum.

The later time with family,
All the stories everyone has to tell
About good times and funny things
That happened to each and every one.

WHAT I DID WHEN I WAS 25

I would go on trips with my mom, dad and sister. We would go to the coast. My dad had a boat in Boothbay Harbor. We would go there for the weekend and stay on the boat. My sister and I would walk around town and go to the taffy place and watch them make it. It was so cool to watch. I would also go candle pin bowling. I wasn't too good at it. The balls were too light. Once in a while, if I was lucky, I would get a strike. I had fun trying, though. I also got to drive my dad's boat. That was really fun.

Beth Compton

THE LITTLE GIRL'S CHRISTMAS

There once was a little girl named Leah. She liked Christmas very much. She went to the mall with her mom. They were walking around when she spotted Santa.

"Can I please tell him what I want for Christmas," she begged. Her mom walked her over to Santa and she went up to him and sat on his lap.

"Hi, Santa."

He looked down at her and asked, "What is your name, little girl?

"My name is Leah."

"Well, Leah, what would you like for Christmas?"

Leah got up close and whispered into Santa's ear, "I would like to have a cat."

She then got off Santa's lap with a big smile on her face. He gave her a candy cane and said, "Merry Christmas."

THE DOG AND THE CAT

There was a dog that liked to go outside and play. One day the dog was wandering around and along came a cat. He went up to the dog. The dog didn't know what to think of the cat. The dog started to walk off, but the cat followed right behind him. When the owner called, the dog ran to him, with the cat chasing closely behind.

The owner said to the dog, "Who is your friend?" Then he looked to see if the cat had any tags, but the cat did not, so the owner took the cat to his home to have supper with the dog.

After the dog and the cat ate supper, they took a nap. When they woke up, they went outside to play until it was time to go to bed. The dog and the cat slept with the owner and became really good friends.

Paul Karwowski (P.K. Allen)

Paul Karwowski (pen name P.K. Allen) was born and raised in New Jersey. After attending college he served in the Navy in Patrol Squadron 26 in Brunswick, Maine. It was in Brunswick that he met his wife of 45 years, Pinky (Margaret). After the service, they got married and eventually built a home in Topsham in 1971, where they raised two boys, Peter and Anthony, and a girl, Amy. Since Amy was handicapped, they became involved with parent groups at Pineland and at the State level.

Amy died in 1996, and Pinky in 2013. Paul now has six wonderful grandchildren. Paul's activities have included camping, white water canoeing, sailing, golf, and family activities. He retired from Bath Iron Works in 2010. He then joined People Plus where he enjoys the Write On! group and Ping Pong, along with his golf and family activities. In 2013, he self-published three books; *REFLECTIONS, Some Thoughts on Life and Love; A JOURNEY; and IMPRESSIONS From an Ordinary Person of Famous People I've Never Met.*

P.K. Allen

THE SEASONS
SPRING

If you like living in a place that has four seasons, then Maine is the place to be. Springtime in Maine can be wet, rainy, muddy, windy, and chilly, with a beautiful day sprinkled here and there, that is, if there isn't a snowstorm. When Pinky and I first moved to Maine, we didn't do much in the early springtime because of the rain and mud or snow. Then, in 1978, we bought an18 ½ foot L.L. Bean ABS canoe. We learned well enough to go whitewater canoeing. We took the boys with us, and they learned quickly. Tony became very proficient and turned out to be an excellent bowman. After a few years, he and I went down the Lower Dead River, 16 miles of class 2 and 3+ rapids. As Tony got older, he went spring skiing and turned out to be a great skier. I, on the other hand, didn't want anything slippery under my feet, just solid ground, so I opted for one week canoe trips with friends every year. Over the years, we made four trips down the St. John River and half-a-dozen trips down the Machias River, and that's not counting the day trips we took down other rivers and streams.

The Winds of Spring

The Spring winds blow briskly
To hustle out Winter's remains,
As chimes clang noisily
Applauding in happy refrains.

The pine trees bend frightfully
Caught in the unyielding gust,
As birds cling tightly to branches
On which they depend and trust.

Tis the way Spring winds blow
To usher in a new season,
And like the changing of the guard
With a purpose and a reason.

It's nature way of telling us
Last year is done and through,
And to set our sights straight ahead
To another that's bright and new.

P.K. Allen

SUMMER

    The summers in Maine are beautiful. The days are long and don't get too hot, except for a week or two at most, and the cool nights make for great sleeping. We never had an air conditioner because we never needed one. We just left all the windows open so the fresh air could blow right through the house. It is unbelievable how many things there are to do in the summertime. You can go to the Lighthouses along the rockbound coast, hike the picturesque mountain trails, shop at L.L. Bean, swim in the ocean, or camp at the wonderful lakes and parks. Did I leave out art galleries, flea markets, museums, and state fairs? I didn't mean to. As a family, over the years, we did all the above, along with our hobbies of gardening, golf, and painting.

Summer Scenes

    The sun shines bright yellow, grass dark green
    Sky painted blue, clouds a white sheen
    Squirrels scurry about, forage for food
    Finches swarm feeders, then home to brood

    Streaks in the sky, planes far away
    Cats hunt field mice, grandchildren play
    Flowers welcome bees, the nectar of life
    Birds sing love songs, the pitch of a fife

    A cool gentle breeze, flag flying free
    Content in the shade, sipping iced tea
    Leaves in trees, sway with the air
    Summer is here, not a worry, not a care

The Summer Wind

    The summer wind blows gently
    Down the hills and leas,
    Kissing each leaf and flower,
    And whispering to bumble bees.

    It carries sweet smells and pollen
    That treat and tickle your nose,
    And lends a feeling of peacefulness
    From your head to the tips of your toes.

P.K. Allen

FALL

    Fall is that time of the year for cool nights, short days, and colorful trees. In our house, it was and still is a time for getting ready for winter. When we had a camper, it was winterized and closed up. We had a wood stove until 1998, so all the wood that was stacked outside had to be brought into the cellar. The remaining vegetables in the garden were picked, and all the patio furniture was stowed away for the winter. We did go for rides and walks in the woods to see the foliage. The colors were stunning. When the children were small, they played soccer. In an election year, if you wanted to meet a local politician running for office, all you had to do was go to the dump on a Saturday morning. You might think that's odd, but that's life in Maine – honest, slow-easy pace. We like to say, "The way life should be."

When Pine Needles Turn Brown

> When pine needles turn brown
>   in the fall of the year,
> The days get shorter,
>   the nights cool and clear.
> The toys from summer
>   are stored neatly away,
> Some birds have gone south
>   while others will stay.
>
> Chipmunks scurry around
>   in search of winter food
> To stuff into their pouches,
>   though not to be rude.
> Split wood from outdoors
>   is stacked in the cellar,
> Maple and oak trees
>   turn bright red and "yeller."
>
> Animals are wary
>   of hunters on the prowl,
> As bird dogs run off
>   to retrieve shot down fowl.
> These are some events
>   this season does crown,
> It's that time of the year
>   when pine needles turn brown.

P.K. Allen

WINTER

Winter is long and very cold in Maine. The days are short, and the nights are long and bitter. It's a great time if you like skiing, snowmobiling, and ice skating. For me, winter is a time for hibernation. I'm just not a winter person. In the early years of our marriage, Pinky and I would take the children to slide and toboggan down some nearby hills. Tony loved the winter. He went skiing as often as he could. I would rather sit by a warm fire and watch a football game of the weekends. Since Pinky didn't like football, she would paint or read or cook. I think the nicest thing about winter is Thanksgiving and Christmas. That is the time we would get together with friends and family.

A Snowflake

A delicate design
    formed by Jack Frost,
    which after completion
    the pattern is lost.

A one of a kind,
    a trillion times dealt,
    to touch the warm ground,
    only to melt.

Winter

I think about moving to another climate
When I retire and start growing old.
For the Winter wind goes right through me
I shiver, my bones getting cold.

I look forward to Spring and Summer
When outside I can dance and play.
They bring me such fond memories.
I think, maybe I'll just stay.

P.K. Allen

WHAT I LIKE MOST ABOUT AMERICA

What I like most about America
    is the people who make her great,
From her busy New York Harbor
    to her misty Golden Gate.

From Hawaii to Alaska,
    from Texas up to Maine,
From Florida to the heartland
    with its amber waves of grain.

From her northern Canadian border states
    To the ones on her Gulf Coast,
From the Atlantic to the Pacific
    live the people of whom I boast.

It's the people of this Country
    of each color, race, and creed,
Who help to build this Nation
    by nurturing freedom's seed.

Yes, it's the people of this country
    of whom I praise and rave,
Because they make this great Nation
    "the land of the free
        and the home of the brave."

P.K. Allen

MY BUCKET LIST

A bucket list is a menu
    of things we'd like to try
While we are still quite able to
    before it's time to die.
So here are some important things
    that I would like to do
Which cannot simply be narrowed down
    as to a number one or two.

To have a cat on my lap
    with my wife by my side,
Grandchildren at my feet
    with smiles in their eyes
Sitting out on the lawn
    where a doe feeds her fawn
Under a bright sunny sky
    where birds sing from on high.
To see the flight of a bee
    and dogs running free
Where the smell in the breeze
    is of flowers and trees
As friends drop on by
    just to say "Hi,"
And Peace all around
    with only Love to be found,
And laughter in the air
    without a worry or a care.

These things on my list
    that are important in my life
Are not made of gold,
    but of family, friends, and wife.
For these are the things
    that make my eyes mist.
These things are first
    on my bucket list.

WHAT IF?

"What if?" is a question we ask
    to explore a different trail,
leaving us to wonder
    whether we'll succeed or fail.

"What if?" is an easy question
    you can answer if you dare.
Just ask yourself these "What ifs?"
    to see how you would fare.

What if I live to be one hundred,
    and outlive my family and friends;
Will I reside in some "old folks home"
    sitting stagnant in my Depends?

What if I have an operation
    that saves my ailing life;
Will I be more compassionate
    or share more with my wife?

What if I become rich and famous,
    and remain in perfect health;
Will I remember where I came from
    or bask in my new wealth?

What if just one if comes true
    and changes my life somehow;
Will I still be the same person
    who is sitting here right now?

"What if?" begs for an answer
    I'm not sure I want to hear.
What makes life so very special
    is to live it without fear.

P.K. Allen

LETTERS

When Pinky was a young girl she was always very inquisitive and outgoing. Things came to her attention that you and I would never have thought of. When she was 11, she wrote to a candy company about their candy bar. She said it seemed the candy bars were getting smaller and smaller. She did get a response from the company. They said that in order to keep quality of the product the same, and not change the price, that reducing the size of the candy bar was a better option.

On another occasion, she wrote to a famous doctor and explained to him that she hated taking needles and if he could please make it easier to take the vaccine. Below is the text of the letter he wrote back to her.

> Dear Margaret:
>
> By now you probably have received your polio inoculation and know that all your fears were for naught. You know now that worrying about how much it was going to hurt was much worse than the momentary prick. I am glad that you were perfectly willing to accept your mother's decision as to what was best for you and, if not already, some time soon you will know how right she was.
>
> Sincerely,
>
> Jonas E. Salk, M. D.
>
> lf

I didn't find his letter until about seven months after Pinky had died. Actually, her uncle found it as he was going through some of her scrapbooks. I had it framed along with the envelope with the 3-cent stamp. It was dated January 26, 1956. I wrote a letter explaining the circumstances and taped it to the back of the frame. Hopefully it will be passed down through generations in the family and will be another possession to remember her by.

P.K. Allen

THE SANDS OF TIME

There's a family tradition we follow
    when someone close has died
To honor that special someone
    with the changing of the tide.

We carve each letter carefully
    with a gentle loving hand,
Spelling out our loved one's name
    in the smoothness of the sand.

We reminisce about the good times
    and chats over a cup of tea
As we sit along the water's edge
    to watch the rising of the sea

As it slowly reclaims each letter,
    embracing a fresh new start,
But it won't erase the memories
    we hold dearly in our hearts.

I AM

I Am the Son of the Father.
I Am the Son of my Mother.
Goodness and Mercy are my sisters.
Mankind is my brother.

In body, I Am the flesh.
In soul, I Am the right.
In morning, I Am the sunrise.
In darkness, I Am the Light.

In heaven, I Am the Holy Spirit.
On earth, I Am the Lamb.
I opened the gates of heaven.
I Am He who is I Am.

P.K. Allen

WINGS

Someone sent me on a journey
To relieve your suffering and pain
And to help with your transition
From life's struggling final refrain.

And though the journey isn't a long one,
You won't be traveling alone.
I'll be there right beside you
On the way to your new home.

SEA OF LOVE

Much like the Glass
    That comes from the Sea
With its surface and edges
    As smooth as can be
Swept by the tide
    And buffed by the sand
Till washed up on shore
    And caressed by a hand

Our love has grown stronger
    And richer thru the years
Seasoned with memories
    Of laughter and tears
Most precious and treasured
    On this we agree
Much like the Glass
    That comes from the Sea

The preceding stories and some poems are excerpts taken from P.K. Allen's next book

The Sands of Time
Life With
and
Life After
Pinky

Julia Garbowski

Julia Garbowski lived on a fruit and vegetable farm in Wisconsin for 27 years. She has recently moved to Maine where her mother and sister live. She has two children, a daughter in Austin, TX and a son in Brooklyn, NY.

She loved writing when she was young and has just started writing again. She writes poetry, short stories, and personal journals. She is really happy to have joined with the Write-On group who have welcomed and encouraged her.

Julia Garbowski

MILK

Within the first four hours, you either suspect, or can clearly see which calves are going to die and which ones are going to fight to live. They were all born in the same barn, with warm gentle mothers standing in patient acceptance of whichever choice they would make. Cows do clean off their babies and encourage them to get up and live, but they are not incessant and vigorous about it like dogs. They do their job in the way of helping, and then they wait. Sometimes the calves act as though they are playing along and seem like they are going to be fine. They get up, they eat, and they even wag their tails a little. If you suspect they are faking it, you watch them over the next few days, maybe talk to them, talk to the mother, and try to convince them they are happy by sending them energy telepathically. But it doesn't work.

I sort of think that the little calves decide somewhere deep inside, (maybe before they are born, or maybe as soon as they take one look at the world), if they will be cows or will turn around and go back to where they came from. I am not completely positive which instinct is more admirable. We seem to appreciate the healthy, lively, and joyous, while we shun the unsure, shrinking, and dying. Maybe those who decide to live validate our own choice to be here one more day.

When the time came, the calf would just stop eating. I am not sure why I felt the need to try to do something every single time. I wanted them all to live. Sometimes the calf would look at me and maybe even try to participate, to do what I was begging it to do. Sometimes the calf would just stare, and only swallow whatever it was unable to let slide out of the sides of its mouth.

I remember realizing that it was a good thing that I had not become a vet after all because I really could not bear it sometimes. I was good at taking charge, too good really. I rubbed vigorously, thinking what to do, and then I would think: if you are not going to do this for yourself, I will do it for you. The warm milk would be all over its neck and my legs as I massaged the throat and the sides of its neck in circles while talking to it. Then somewhere in there I always realized it was not up to me. You can do it, I would say... Please, I would say... It will be all right, I would promise. Sometimes it worked.

I love the smell of cattle. And I love the gorgeous huge nostrils and the sight of the huge tongue going up into the entrance of the nostrils without going inside. I love the place on the side of the face where the wet nose meets the fur. There is a little indentation right there in a certain spot that is perfect for a kiss. I would kiss it sometimes as an apology, sometimes in appreciation, and sometimes as a good bye. I would always smell it, bringing the scent into me while I tried from the outside to connect to the inside of the creature.

THE SPACE BETWEEN

The space between raindrops and

between conversations,

invisible particles

landing as a solid,

separate and new,

unerasable.

Julia Garbowski

CLICHÉ WOMAN

Some people hate clichés. They are like fingernails on a chalkboard. They are also hard to swallow, and rub us the wrong way. I think they are like the processed food of ideas.

This morning I am realizing how much I contain these groups of words, - boiled down ideas with no meaning left. I am at the end of my rope, need to find my Achilles heel, bat ideas around, stop barking up the wrong tree, call a spade a spade, change my tune, and get with the program - I guess I had better nip this in the bud and stop listing them.

I talk about how I write some good stuff and some garbage, and that I am comfortable with that. Sometimes I don't know which is which. Last night, I dreamed that my body was full of garbage. It was literal gooey, smelly, crumpled garbage, but what is the difference, really? I am full of garbage. I put it in my mouth, take it in with all of my senses, create it, and probably was born full of it. She is full of garbage. She is full of it. She is full of shit. She is beautiful. Can an individual word like beautiful be a cliché? It has no meaning, really.

Lately, a message all around us is that the root of all evil is self-hatred. Personally, I think too much self-exploration and inward looking and seeking is ridiculous. I admit I am fully engaged in it at the moment because I have lost control of my life and think that I might be able to control something. At the same time, thinking too much is just plain bad. My grandmother used to tell me that we are here to do what we know, not what we think is right. When we stop to think of what the rule is, we are lost. I also don't think we have to, or maybe are even supposed to, understand ourselves fully.

One of the things I loved about riding my horse, Chinook, was that the experience was a union of forces, mine and his. I almost always rode him bareback. I could just grab the bridle from the hook in the barn and run out to the pasture in my bare feet and call him. He was a perfect Chestnut, 14-hand Quarter horse, and I could jump right up on him from the ground. We became one together, moving where we both wanted to go, and it was no big deal. It could be a 20 minute walk, or it could be a full gallop

Julia Garbowski

across the field. In that act, I was not in control, and it felt right.

Things do not feel right lately. So, I am looking inside trying to find the garbage and throw it out. I am thinking about what I should be. Some people are telling how much I could be, if I would just... do what I am supposed to do. But the truth is, all of those images of what I think I am supposed to do that are appealing, are merely false, superficial images. Like clichés, they tell me something important, but that is only part of the whole. What is worse is that they are so pervasive that the whole actually disappears. That's it. I am trying to be a cliché. I am nothing, but I will become something. I will cast out the garbage, heal myself, set my sights on clear goals, and voila!, I can be a cliché. I will just have the appearance of a woman without being one.

So, today, since hope springs eternal, instead of being stressed out, pinning my hopes, grasping at straws, or shooting for the moon, I will remember what I love, including looking at what I love about garbage, and I will know that I do not need to be healed to be whole.

And, I will save one penny for your thoughts.

Julia Garbowski

THE ASSENTOR

We were both the same height and weight, and walked arm in arm, talking and singing together, as though we were one person thinking out loud. Victoria had a musical way of saying my name that made me feel very beautiful. Our bodies were calling out to be women instead of girls but still craving the adventures of children. We sneaked out of our houses for midnight walks to the beach, and when brave, we climbed the breakwater rocks out into the cove.

People who lived in the old whaling town held a reverence for ancestors, ghosts, an ocean full of fish, and historic houses. I did not know that it was unusual to see large sculptures in yards, windmills at the end of a wharf, fishing boats moored next to yachts, men holding hands with each other, or movie theaters for international films.

We knew that somewhere far away, probably in Mississippi, and of course, Africa, there were poor people. Starving even. Maybe naked and with no shoes. But we believed that our generation would end poverty. Not so far away, in the Bronx, children were shooting each other, and little bags of drugs were being exchanged in school yards as replacements for love. We believed that our generation would heal the addicts.

We talked about it, and could see it, with the clearness of young eyes. We knew that all people would soon be sharing together in providing for each other as one family of man. After all, we believed that there were only three things people needed from the outer world: food, a warm bed, and art. And we would love everyone. All of this ending, healing, beginning, would just unfold easily, with no fighting.

****

Julia Garbowski

I have no memory of this story, but my grandmother often spoke of me, before the age of two, coming into the house from the back yard with what she called "a load in my pants." Grams had taken me by the hand to go upstairs and cheerfully change my diaper. A neighbor was visiting sitting at the kitchen table and made some kind of remark and a disapproving sound when we walked past her. Evidently, I turned around and looked her squarely in the eyes and said loudly, "I don't like you either."

The first time I really remember a bully was when a kid was picking on my younger sister. He used to slap her when he walked by, shout, "Weeeeeeiiiiirrdddooooo," from far down the hall, or point at her and laugh. One day I was walking down the hallway and saw my sister sitting on the floor in front of a locker. The door was open, and she sort of had her head leaning inside. I stopped to see if she needed help finding something and discovered that she was sobbing into the metal compartment, trying to hide tears. He had just kicked her in the back. When I put my arms around her, I could feel a deep shaking coming from within that entered my body and carried me up and into the nearby lunchroom looking for him.

It was a beautiful old gym with warm wood floors and a high stage. Lunch tables filled the gym floor and were also up on the stage. The bully was walking up the steps to go to a table on the stage. I did not take the stairs but jumped up onto the stage and cut him off before he sat down. I vaguely remember grabbing a handful of shirt in my fist about where a heart should have been. Mostly, I remember looking deeply into gray eyes, and telling him never to touch my sister again. I meant it with all of who I was. I have no idea what I thought I would do if he did ever touch her again, but somehow I knew he wouldn't.

****

Julia Garbowski

Victoria went away to college and sent me hundreds of letters over four years. She danced, traveled, studied art, and became a gentle teacher. A man with thick black hair, brown shoulders and arms, and blue eyes, asked me to marry him, crawl along the ground picking strawberries and beans, and throw burlap bags full of sweet corn up onto a truck. It sounded like heaven to me.

There are still people in Mississippi and Africa and in every city and town in the country who have too little to eat, too many guns, and many more little bags of poisonous comfort. We are not providing enough food, beds, or art.

****

There have been many bullies since then: one behind a counter, another in a school, a doctor at a hospital, and a voice coming across the phone from miles away... The young girl who jumped up on the stage was no great hero, but she did not run away. She had a righteous clarity about what she believed. The adult she became learned that the righteous are dangerous, so she suspended her judgments, began to assent, and chooses to say something meaningless and nice, unclench her fist, and walk away.

In the morning there is coffee, a little dog to let outside and small decisions about the small ways I spend my day.

Patty LaDean Sparks

Patty was born in Bath, Maine, the "City of Ships," in 1946, adopted 9 days later, and raised in Brunswick.

Recipient of the prestigious Thalhimer's Women's Studies Essay Writers Scholarship, she attended the University of Richmond in Virginia.

Patty is currently focusing on her first book:
From, The Servant's Daughter, A Poetic Journal From Early Maine Life.

She resides near the shores of her beloved Maquoit Bay. Active in her community, she also delights in being "Mum" to two pure white feral cats, ABIATHAR and HUBERT, and "Mems" to one exceptionally talented grandchild, Gabrielle LaDean.

Patty LaDean Sparks

HAIKU

Haiku is the most internationally recognizable of Japanese poetic forms. Haiku poems are composed of seventeen-syllables, arranged in the form of three lines 5-7-5 syllables each. They usually focus on the natural world and the seasons, but many poets also use them to capture the fleeting human experience.

THE MESSENGER

Red breasted Robin
black eyes upon me glaring
pose: on hues of spring

LOVE & LONGING

I wake in the night
reach for you there beside me
finding the sheets... cold

AT
DAWN

Old eyes gaze sea-ward
she rises and combs her hair
a woman...alone

Patty LaDean Sparks

BUTTERFLY DANCER

There once was a butterfly
so fragile, so Devine
who needed some rest
but hey...that was fine

Her wings did not move
she appeared in a trance
then suddenly butterfly
started to prance

Tiny legs started dancing
no longer could she hide
for this was her gift
drawn deep from inside

Oh, it turned out to be
such a magical jig
to the left she would zag
and the right she would zig

She finished her boogie
that bright summer's day
and I laughed, as she
flew-off my sleeve...
and away!

Patty LaDean Sparks

UNTITLED DIALOG

"Is it still raining, my love?"

"Yes dear, I am afraid it is."

"Oh well."

"Yes, oh well in deed, and I am bored to death with it.
Bored to death with this place.
Bored to death with this life.
Bored to death with myself."

"What did you say, dear?"

"Nothing...of any consequence."
"NOTHING.:

WINTER SOLSTICE

Come, celebrate the Goddess
who shrouds the sun in shades
of grey and the moon behind
shadowy white fingers of silence.

The snowy white gown, spun from
breathless orbs of ice, swirls across
a barren landscape, blanketing all
beneath its graceful dance. She
laughs, then sighs, and ancient symbols
crystalize on frosted windowpanes.

Open the door daughters of light.
Come sing, dance, celebrate, for this
is a magical time. Reflect, release, restore
and renew, for a gorgeous winter guest from
afar has swept in.

Patty LaDean Sparks

TWILIGHT

"Come forth!"
bewitching hour tis
ALL HALLOWS EVE
at
last.

SPECTER'S TROD
your night till
dawn's first light
from their realm
'twixt
present
and
past.

HAIKU FROM THE HEART

THE DECISION

"No!" the demon wails,
"Writers are born, not chosen!"
I...take up my pen

ROBERTA'S SONG

Ninety year old eyes
for the first time met her child's
closure...was love's gift

SEAWEED

Greenish-grey beauty
cast up by a lonely sea
blackens on the sands.

Patty LaDean Sparks

AUTUMNAL BEING

The real
harvest of contentment
waits to be gathered in.

The smells of hearth
fires burning,
Chilly evenings,
that bring a wondrous
night's sleep,
while crunching leaves under
foot, all hasten
the call.

Autumn's
beauty beckons us,
"Come...partake of my generous
bounty!"

MY "MAYBE" VIEW

Maybe, it's time that the world
wants something better

Maybe, we have a problem
making things right

Maybe, our time is running out
on just how to fix things

Maybe, I'm wrong but,
Maybe...Maybe, I'm
right!

Patty LaDean Sparks

JANUARY

Come,
Let winter
weave
Her
wondrous
spell,
for all
of
nature
is at
peace,
in this
the
month
of
dreams

HAIKU FOR A WINTER SOUL

MAINE NOR'EASTER

Seas rage, winds pummel
shorelines of granite and pine
as snow...falls on snow.

WINTER ECHO

Evergreens...moaning
swaying to frozen music
sung by northeast winds.

Patty LaDean Sparks

**THE
SERENADE**

Tis "somewhere" so distant
ever so small

Piercing the "stillness"
with its ancient call

Quiet breaths softly
rise and fall

As the white-throated
Sparrow beckons
to all.

MAINE SUMMER SOLITUDE

I shall
carry out
my tea tray
prop old pillows
up against a tree
creating a
"lounge"
upon the earth

There,
thru eyelids
longing to close
I'll await the elusive
"kiss"
of an August breeze
against my cheek

Then,
into blissful
surrender as the
breath rises and falls
my soul shall
drift down,
down,
down into
the quiet
"solitude"
of a perfect
summer
day

ABOUT WRITE ON!

In 1995 Jean Martz, along with a few other people with an interest in writing, decided to form a writing group to develop their mutual interests in expressing their feelings through the written word. Thus was born Write On! of People Plus in Brunswick, Maine. Today the group numbers over 20 active members having diverse interests and talents who take joy in writing and sharing expressions and feelings with each other on a weekly basis throughout the year. If you have such an interest, come join us.

Members of Write On! at their weekly Wednesday meeting on April 16, 2014.

INDEX

Title	Page	Author
1941 Oldsmobile	58	Wendell Kinney
A Charming Old Cottage	105	Winnie Silverman
A Dark Stormy Night	141	Beth Compton
A Day's Catch	132	Margie Kivel
A Snowflake	148	P.K. Allen
A Song I Heard in Maine	75	Adelaide Guernelli
A Street Grows Up	110	Winnie Silverman
A Summer Place	116	Karen Schneider
A Tail of Two Parents	78	Ann Robinson
A Tree Grows in Cleveland	111	Winnie Silverman
A Tribute to "My Dads"	68	Gladys Szabo
Against the Gray	133	Margie Kivel
At Dawn	164	Patty Sparks
At Last	29	Bonnie Wheeler
Autumnal Being	168	Patty Sparks
Back to Boston—May 2013	5	Charlotte Hart
Becoming Invisible	40	Elizabeth King
Be Careful What You Wish For	124	Vince McDermott
Bobby's Special Christmas	141	Beth Compton
Brunswick in December	8	Charlotte Hart
Butterfly Dancer	165	Patty Sparks
Camp Sunshine	102	Nancy Sohl
Cliché Woman	158	Julia Garbowski
Cloud Dreaming	134	Margie Kivel
Cold Moonlight	121	Vince McDermott
Conversation Between Two 21st Century Teens	88	Ralph Laughlin
Doggone	80	Ann Robinson
Dunbar B & B	60	Wendell Kinney
Fall	147	P.K. Allen
For This One Day	50	Dottie Moody
Grandmothers	42	Elizabeth King
Grandpa's Farm	34	Bonnie Wheeler
Groundhog	123	Vince McDermott

INDEX

Title	Page	Author
Haiku	164	Patty Sparks
Heat of Crystallization	40	Elizabeth King
He's Beautiful	49	Dottie Moody
Holiday Wishes to the WRITE ON! Group	27	Bob Dow
I Am	31	Bonnie Wheeler
I Am	41	Elizabeth King
I Am	153	P.K. Allen
I Can't Believe Everything I Know	87	Ralph Laughlin
I Think	88	Ralph Laughlin
I Wrote a Poem	119	Vince McDermott
January	169	Patty Sparks
Kittie	52	Dottie Moody
Letters	152	P.K. Allen
Life and Death	75	Adelaide Guernelli
Living in Maine	86	Ralph Laughlin
Lost Pictures	55	Dottie Moody
Love and Longing	164	Patty Sparks
Love at First Sight	71	Gladys Szabo
Love Out Loud	31	Bonnie Wheeler
Loving Memories of Aunt Ethel	72	Gladys Szabo
Maine Nor'easter	169	Patty Sparks
Maine Summer Solitude	171	Patty Sparks
March Comes in ----	40	Elizabeth King
Math of Emotions	87	Ralph Laughlin
Memorial Day	26	Bob Dow
Migration	43	Elizabeth King
Milk	155	Julia Garbowski
Morning-After Ghosts	135	Margie Kivel
Morning Serenity	69	Gladys Szabo
Mother's Day Reflections	73	Gladys Szabo
My "Maybe" View	168	Patty Sparks
My Bucket List	150	P.K. Allen
My Child	38	Bonnie Wheeler

INDEX

Title	Page	Author
My Daughter, Kate	113	Karen Schneider
My Grandfather	2	Charlotte Hart
My Thursday Letter	32	Bonnie Wheeler
New Family Member	65	Gladys Szabo
October Flush	137	Margie Kivel
Ode to a Husband	93	Ralph Laughlin
Oh, My Aching Back	63	Wendell Kinney
Once	115	Karen Schneider
Only One at a Time	76	Adelaide Guernelli
Party Politic Pox	92	Ralph Laughlin
Peace	51	Dottie Moody
Penny the Sneaky Cat	142	Beth Compton
People Watching (While on Parade)	25	Bob Dow
Remember When	98	Nancy Sohl
Roberta's Song	167	Patty Sparks
Sacred Space	47	Dottie Moody
Sea of Love	154	P.K. Allen
Seaweed	167	Patty Sparks
Sebago Lake on the Fourth of July	3	Charlotte Hart
Sermons or Poetry?	48	Dottie Moody
Signs of the Times	24	Bob Dow
Snow Day	103	Nancy Sohl
Snowfall	95	Ralph Laughlin
Sound Mind	38	Bonnie Wheeler
Solstice	44	Elizabeth King
Southern Comfort and Northern Bliss	30	Bonnie Wheeler
Spirit of Christmas	84	Ann Robinson
Spring	94	Ralph Laughlin
Spring	145	P.K. Allen
Step by Step	136	Margie Kivel
Strawberry Season	123	Vince McDermott
Summer	146	P.K. Allen
Summer Scenes	146	P.K. Allen

INDEX

Title	Page	Author
Tell Me How You Came to Be	138	Margie Kivel
Thanksgiving	142	Beth Compton
Thanksgiving Day	75	Adelaide Guernelli
The Accidental Hooker	70	Gladys Szabo
The Adventures of Sir Snidely	126	Vince McDermott
The Assentor	160	Julia Garbowski
The Bear Who Came to My House	129	Karen Johnson
The Best Gift of All	97	Nancy Sohl
The Argument In Favor of Accumulative Materialism	89	Ralph Laughlin
The Blizzard of 1977	66	Gladys Szabo
The Bottom of the Fifth	26	Bob Dow
The Decision	167	Patty Sparks
The Deer Whisperer	7	Charlotte Hart
The Dog and the Cat	143	Beth Compton
The Future	27	Bob Dow
The Leonids	44	Elizabeth King
The Little Girl's Christmas	143	Beth Compton
The Little Things in Life	99	Nancy Sohl
The Messenger	164	Patty Sparks
The Moonlit Night	141	Beth Compton
The Nest	73	Gladys Szabo
The Sands of Time	153	P.K. Allen
The Seasons of our Lives	100	Nancy Sohl
The Serenade	170	Patty Sparks
The Space Between	157	Julia Garbowski
The Storm	122	Vince McDermott
The Summer Wind	146	P.K. Allen
The Sunday Tradition	114	Karen Schneider
The Twenty	91	Ralph Laughlin
The Undecorated Tree	36	Bonnie Wheeler
The White Pigeon of Battery Park	11	Ruth Foehring
The Winds of Spring	145	P.K. Allen
Time	56	Dottie Moody

INDEX

Title	Page	Author
Together	18	Ruth Foehring
To India	53	Dottie Moody
Tribute to "My Dads"	68	Gladys Szabo
Twilight	167	Patty Sparks
Ultimate Responsibility	95	Ralph Laughlin
Uncle Benny's Visit	120	Vince McDermott
Untitled Dialogue	166	Patty Sparks
Veterans Day and a Bike Chained to a Tree	6	Charlotte Hart
Wedding in the Mountains of Stow, Maine	4	Charlotte Hart
Weekend Ritual	139	Margie Kivel
What Have I Done?	54	Dottie Moody
What If?	151	P.K. Allen
What is Poetry? (and the Rhymer's Response)	23	Bob Dow
What I Did When I was 25	142	Beth Compton
What I Like Most About America	149	P.K. Allen
Where Has America Gone	90	Ralph Laughlin
Where is Dave Slovenski?	9	Charlotte Hart
Who Understands?	33	Bonnie Wheeler
Wings	154	P.K. Allen
Winter	148	P.K. Allen
Winter (poem)	148	P.K. Allen
Winter Candy	134	Margie Kivel
Winter Echo	169	Patty Sparks
Winter Solstice	166	Patty Sparks
Womankind	31	Bonnie Wheeler
Write On	46	Dottie Moody

Made in the USA
Charleston, SC
31 July 2014